WE LESSER
GODS

ELIZABETH CLAYTON

authorHOUSE®

AuthorHouse™
1663 Liberty Drive
Bloomington, IN 47403
www.authorhouse.com
Phone: 1 (800) 839-8640

Published by AuthorHouse   03/08/2016

ISBN: 978-1-5049-7550-6 (sc)
ISBN: 978-1-5049-7583-4 (hc)
ISBN: 978-1-5049-7584-1 (e)

Library of Congress Control Number: 2016901525

Print information available on the last page.

All appointments to the text of We Lesser Gods *are photographs of Elizabeth's personal works; the photography and other matters where assisted throughout by Tonia Germany with Ora Steele.*

This book is printed on acid-free paper.

Contents

A Prefacing Addendum to the work "We Lesser Gods"

A "quiet adequate" addendum is near completion, to accompany the work presented here, behind, "We Lesser Gods," the addendum to be published in early summer 2016. These verses are predominantly from the year 2013, with some few others of various subjects and themes, therefore not appropriate to present a fifth portion – truly the full theme was during its developing, its struggle, into the "travail" of expression. It was just igniting, thrusting, connecting into understanding. It was, to be most correct, a transitional record of thought.

I did not like the work I was producing, feeling a different kind of catharsis and instruction, even leaning back into 2012. I did not feel happy and expressive, but rather pressed and expressive. The themes are arranged often and again, to "being" – not so much recalling what had already been or mourning the denouement and conclusion of tomorrow, allthewhile extolling their glory. The moment moved into place and dissonance began its full assault. The folder was laid aside although I continued in this portion but consciously working back to earlier themes, expressions and conclusions.

The content of the 2013 verses calls for different vocabulary, sentence structure, figures of speech, and less description of the physical world and much more of the psychological. Most, of course, the thematic ponderings, jousting's, and sparring offered grave dissonance, constricting, or rather drawing a most unaltaring, gray ambiance of fear and powerlessness. I felt no longer a poet, but a writer, a dark writer, of verse prose. Rhythm was kept in pleasantness, but qualities of spontaneous expression – so much necessary in much poetry, was not accessible and I grieved this lost part. I just could not know with what malady I wrestled.

Still, at times, I would return, briefly to my old self with a burst of beauty and good, if naive, fanciful, "Cinderella-like," the passion flower responding to the warmth of its lord.

Throughout 2012-2013, many incidents occurred, each requiring adjustments and reasoning - as in a year of the lives of us all, especially the full onset of rheumatoid arthritis. Truly, for me, the entire was the maturing that comes to those who live into a near fullness. I believe by portion four of "We Lesser Gods," I evidence a much more successful transitioning than when I began in 2012-2014, as well as a writer, however the mighty of the struggle.

We can learn from any experience, if we allow our ableness, and the struggle of the two years, primarily 2013, was a lesson well taught, although still incomplete, but as was, hopefully learned well. But I was still more often than not, displeased with my poems, deciding to omit them in the work of "We Lesser Gods."

I wish the addendum to reflect these sentiments and embellish the better aspects of the piece, *"We Lesser Gods."* I still find great joy in beauty, in the grand Natural, in special, if a smaller number, of relationships, but perhaps more - as father Porphias noted in his work *"Wounded by Love:"* "What the bird said to me, that it 'did not say'." (speaking of time spent in solitude and thought.)

The I-Thou principle has been my "sack of stones" all of my life, interwoven with ability, special aptitudes, and a childhood of abject poverty, although guided by highly motivated, able parents of fundamental beliefs. My Bipolar illness has added great introspection and extremes of mood balance have made the inevitable progress of the walk of life to become more desperate, for a satisfactory conclusion. All of "that" is somewhat relieved now through my pen, my brushes, clay, the needle, and realizing, as most do who take time from noise and activity that "man is the only animal who knows that someday he will die," so poignantly expressed by the marvelous German poet,

Holderlin, who died in an asylum in England in 1843, having suffered from acute depression all his life.

One clarifying construct should be included here: to those who are truly Bipolar, "everything" that is thought, felt - perceived - is processed in the extreme. There is no medias, no middle, no average. This attending quality may be expressed in very different fashions. Therefore, my doubt and questions, my intense escape into beauty, have always been with me, attached even more to beauty, the whole of which is my antidote to despair.

Life is an experience of moments, felt throughout of our cognitive collections and these subjects washed through heavily or lightly by meanings of our senses. With all, there are questions and answers and the true reality, at times, is that there are simply some questions that have no answers, this albatross, for me, of "must" fundamental, known certainty finally freeing as it fell into the sea of acceptance and hope. We must be attended by the truism that every moment is not "sweetness and light," but difficult - at times, so as to be "hurted to our hearts," but put in perspective, whether out of resignation, defensive posturing or reacting - through "mental gymnastics" as Freud so well addressed our "adjustment process" - or desperation of circumstances we cannot even begin to understand, such as faith and trust; we can find that we can all experience cups that "runneth over". There is always enough in what is left.

Elizabeth
completed at noontime
November 20, 2015

Chaos\Pandamonium

Being\Existance without God

A Pensive Accompaniment
We Do Not Bow

Silence rings throughout, intense, small bells,
together, saying my ever loneliness – now my emptiness, and
reticently appraised, resignation.
Perhaps a better semantic knowing of this
present sentiment would be merely acceptance of
familiar scapes – steps, sounds – all that
are easily, and therefore more comfortably,
traversed.
Did passion and wonder pass with the days,
their complextions, in the hours, sometimes
lost to holding – or did there come a
reasoning that our time in conscious awareness
can only yield such – passing, onward
into the outward, a "casting off,"
accompanying.
Such gifts provide the construct of yesterday,
sweet moments and appreciative
gatherings – what can, forming the feast.
Sunlight reaches, always, by the path of the moon
and stars, into, ever, the dawn, pebbles,
sand grains – bells – not requiring, as we continue.
Thenso, our walk is not so difficult, into the away;
we are castaways by our own hands, and so,
beautifully fatigued.
There is no passage after winter, only as to decline
the spring, as does the journeyman.

Hymns can be sung, and movement can be, smiles
expressed, and truth offered, but shadows
have the press of natural law.

That we continue is noble, that we look to the feast, sacred,
and of it all, in the shadowing of our steps is a
kind gesture, that we twine out the bramble.

Standing tall, able, bathed and balmed, we, the "lesser gods"
we surely be; yet, in the visiting of deepest night –
– we do not bow.

Elizabeth

in deepest night, an hour in early morning –
February 11, 2013

celebrating, in verse fashion, the walk we all make,
if we are gifted the pleasure – not to be
spent, at day's end –

not a rationalization, but only an humble appraisal of
the reality that is, objectivly –

an elizabeth afterthought –

Foreword
Ulysses

It little profits that an idle king,
By this still hearth, among these barren crags,
Match'd with an aged wife, I mete and dole
Unequal laws unto a savage race,
That hoard, and sleep, and feed, and know not me.

I cannot rest from travel: I will drink
Life to the lees: All times I have enjoy'd
Greatly, have suffer'd greatly, both with those
That loved me, and alone, on shore, and when
Thro' scudding drifts the rainy Hyades
Vext the dim sea: I am become a name;
For always roaming with a hungry heart
Much have I seen and known; cities of men
And manners, climates, councils, governments,
Myself not least, but honour'd of them all;
And drunk delight of battle with my peers,
Far on the ringing plains of windy Troy.
I am a part of all that I have met;
Yet all experience is an arch wherethro'
Gleams that untravell'd world whose margin fades
For ever and forever when I move.
How dull it is to pause, to make an end,
To rust unburnish'd, not to shine in use!
As tho' to breathe were life! Life piled on life
Were all too little, and of one to me
Little remains: but every hour is saved
From that eternal silence, something more,
A bringer of new things; and vile it were
For some three suns to store and hoard myself,
And this gray spirit yearning in desire

To follow knowledge like a sinking star,
Beyond the utmost bound of human thought.

This is my son, mine own Telemachus,
To whom I leave the sceptre and the isle,—
Well-loved of me, discerning to fulfil
This labour, by slow prudence to make mild
A rugged people, and thro' soft degrees
Subdue them to the useful and the good.
Most blameless is he, centred in the sphere
Of common duties, decent not to fail
In offices of tenderness, and pay
Meet adoration to my household gods,
When I am gone. He works his work, I mine.

There lies the port; the vessel puffs her sail:
There gloom the dark, broad seas. My mariners,
Souls that have toil'd, and wrought, and thought with me—
That ever with a frolic welcome took
The thunder and the sunshine, and opposed
Free hearts, free foreheads—you and I are old;
Old age hath yet his honour and his toil;
Death closes all: but something ere the end,
Some work of noble note, may yet be done,
Not unbecoming men that strove with Gods.
The lights begin to twinkle from the rocks:
The long day wanes: the slow moon climbs: the deep
Moans round with many voices. Come, my friends,
'Tis not too late to seek a newer world.
Push off, and sitting well in order smite
The sounding furrows; for my purpose holds
To sail beyond the sunset, and the baths

Of all the western stars, until I die.
It may be that the gulfs will wash us down:
It may be we shall touch the Happy Isles,
And see the great Achilles, whom we knew.
Tho' much is taken, much abides; and tho'
We are not now that strength which in old days
Moved earth and heaven, that which we are, we are;
One equal temper of heroic hearts,
Made weak by time and fate, but strong in will
To strive, to seek, to find, and not to yield.

Alfred Lord Tennyson
*One of the two "giant" poets of the British Victorian period
(the extended reign of Queen Victoria)*

From *The Divine Comedy*

Shipmates, I said, who through a hundred thousand
perils have reached the West, do not deny
to the brief remainingwatch our senses stand
experience of the world beyond the sun.
Greeks! You were not born to live like brutes,
but to press on toward manhood and recognition!
With this brief exhortation I made my crew
so eager for the voyage I could hardly
have held them back from it when I was through;
and turning our stern toward morning, our bow toward night,
we bore southwest out of the world of man;
we made wings of our oars for our fool's flight.
That night we raised the other pole ahead
with all its stars, and ours had so declined
it did not rise out of its ocean bed.
Five times since we had dipped our bending oars
beyond the world, the light beneath the moon
had waxed and waned, when dead upon our course
we sighted, dark in space, a peak so tall
I doubted any man had seen the like.
Our cheers were hardly sounded, when a squall
broke hard upon our bow from the new land:
three times it sucked the ship and the sea about
as it pleased Another to order and command.
At the fourth, the poop rose and the bow went down
till the sea closed over us and the light was gone.

Dante; The Divine Comedy. Inferno. Canto XXVI
Dante: one of the world's sixth most worthy
poets – of the medieval period;
The Divine Comedy, part Inferno, Canto XXVI -
the death of Ulysses in hell.

Acknowledgments

Acknowledgments are often expressed when
assistance -- effort, inspiration,
encouragement -- are extended to an individual, or
small number of participants by a larger group --
or at times, by a single person or circumstance.

Verses contained in this work, "We Lesser Gods," were written
over an almost three-year period (2013-present), under my own
hand, alone; a third portion to be published at a later time.

However, the decision to publish these present verses was sudden,
without any truly, engaging thought, requiring,
then, much work -- productive activity --
within a small window of hours.

Therefore, my truest measure of gratitude is offered
to Ora Steele, a long-time friend and also
a very able typist, with many other valuable attributes.

Tonia Germany, who has been with me in my past
several books, is responsible for finishing the entire
manuscript for publication -- my true "girl Friday."

This small couplet, who worked under press, always deferring to me,
enabled the work to become processed -- rapidly -- from an
idea -- very different from my other work --
to its reality, one I offer, happily,
to my readers.
--a stem, and two roses -- salute!

Elizabeth
October 17, 2015
eleven -fifteen pm

Preface

Writing is not a structure, a constant flow – a field of Goldenrod, a touch across – and without apology, and with a merely small explanation – it is all of these, in the abstract – yet probably, and possibly, can be made the concrete, within the self, when expressed ably, with genuine intent, and in wishful communication, through the phenomenon of semantics, if, yet, with their inabilities; the thoughts of the most magnanimously gifted, the bestowed with most wealth as the penning wordsmith – it is he who becomes a seminal mind of his century.

We can, in most instances, speak audibly that which we feel, or know, but in moments of carated sentiment, silent statements between souls are more effective, superlative to all that is truly known; in such rare, truly epic circumstances, the pen cannot best this sensing, intuiting arrangement. Only consideration and understanding of that written, or heard, of it is let to suffice.

Past this exception, we may review the years after formal study and learning, when writing becomes more a vehicle which carries information, and very little sentiment. The world of work is requiring, but still numerous instances arrive of "woven" relationships which involve feelings too tender to be adequately expressed – or conversely, too negative to include emotionally. In addition, necessary strength and resolve are often lacking, or are found too weak to produce\declare a decision.

Playfully, suggestively, humorously – or with condolences – or congratulations and praise – these arenas are still in place within our repertoire, but appreciation is easily overlooked, and sentiments that plague our psyches are too often left silent, whether written or spoken; the arts of reading and listening, are faring very poorly in the present. Color, movement, and sound very often take away incidental learning, transferring, and associations; insight is overlooked by the next, upcoming frame – one which very well could suggest ideas,

values, and principles necessary to health adjustment – but more, that which celebrates the unhealthy.

…silent by pen or strength of voice – records of moments, events, with fiefdoms and castles, mansions and cabins – down their halls of details – in whatever dimension – that passed, the spontaneously now –or those portions of earth and heaven out which come whispering questions which we know have not any answers in any known realm – to which we can accommodate: these boundaries, all when worded, continue to comprise the unnumbered volumes which rest comfortably or ill, in all manner of settings. Visuals, today, make acquiring information more easily, if, often times, ineffectively, done, but learning cannot always be "fun," although in many very important areas of study; they are completely necessary, to enhance, and not only to supplement the entire process: the "fun" is in the combining together of all the consistencies of the complete exchange!

With these remarks – they being an unhappy word usage, unspoken words, additionally, alongside some opinion and position, the gift of words is, of course, descriptively endless; and when we are unable to use them effectively to present the feast of life, to encourage going to table, - often – our lives will know, at least in part, a wholeness.

My life has been – all of my life – primarily cathartic although the celebration of beauty, no matter the arrangement, other than the must producing of good, has been my most conscious joy, more at various moments, behaviorally, censorial, or insightfully understood moods accompanying these varied experiences, these coloring the entire milieu of the wide expanse of affectation – the desire for "must good" should be explained, clearly – the avoidance of conflict and angst – not a necessary righteousness or piety – such would bring a negatively attached valence to all in conjunction with my personal fencing with words.

If perfect restoration can occur, scars are often left underneath, unpleasant reminders of the once hurt or wound – a wish to prevent an unhappy fear come together, again of circumstance, either mortal or

immortal, or with a reprieve of hope, hanging about, hope, and with both, once reconstruction has occurred, as if that of both.

There is that which can be and there is that which cannot. In my most honest corner of conscious thought, combined with sentiments too complicated by modernity, greater even than to taste a brief discussion, we are at once the blessed of celestial light, and shadowed by mortal senses and hope.

Being that we consider, in our I-Thou centras, unknown – and finding that we have daily evidence – consensus is too varied, multi-faceted, convoluted, unknown – other than in acute individual perception: all –how more than surmise, speculation – backward to myth intertwined with reality.

Not being a student of religion and theology, formally, but in my life, both spectator and participant – these words merely become individual musings, but they are genuine ruminations of soulful introspection. We do wish to, and reconstruct so, that no error has ever occurred. Such is the record of my work; we all, however, look to the new day and its gifts – Pippa may pass by with her innocent melody – but when the signs of westward dim begin to appear, we face, always, conclusion. Details, as Balzac so expressively demonstrates in his descriptions – merely a drying puddle of street water – such colors all that we record: the hinder-hours, and paths, the glory – the ecstasy of the moment, the idle fancies of promise – still, just the suggestion of hours in the unchared offing – the grail – in perhaps, the tomorrow – knowing, althewhile, with the advent of abstract thought, that beside the new blossom, gifted of the darkened separation of night, lie those others, lifeless, having lived their day, spent their final sweetness, complete; their petals, yet, wet with the still, instinctive struggling life.

I cannot disassociate my joy of the moment from its individual identity – its passing into conclusion, containing, yet, a portion of its present being. This darkness, though, perhaps some manifestation of an unfortunate, neurotic leaving of childhood, or a suggested, arrested adolescence, this

darkness has been within my spirit since memory – as a determined, gray pall, a dust of moving, ever angst.

Andso, these later verses, quite following many "normal" days and nights of glorious experience, risk-taking, wounding repentance (having a fundamentalist religious education) – pouring innocent, naïve good – these verses leaning heavily into preoccupation with conclusion, or aspects of life which foster it – these have stood lieutenant to my attention.

Voluminous verses have been written, in numerous fashions, languages, of nearly all, and in the widest of the spectrum of circumstances – the subject of significance, either veiled or no: it is in its whole being the pearl, the crown – the grail we wish and work toward, to be set aside in time – a short time, extending centuries, yet eons, but within time – the constant of all – inside we "lesser gods."

The ambiance of this work is the flow of beauty, with all of its negative attendants, yet the good into the great separation of which the mystic, dervish poet, Rumi, so beautifully speaks. As was my always, I can be only me – and I, of we "lesser gods," can only accept. We do not "bow out" as does the British "pagan poet," A. Swinburne, in his garden verse – or place all negatives into a bag without further thought by simply parroting "God will take care of all of us" (a friend of great wisdom) – My center of truth is stated through these verses, here acknowledging doubt, faith, uncertainty, and gratitude: "Paradox" is a convenient word for simply seeing "things" which do not balance correctly, into opposition, in our own, personal perception (a matter of great speculation, including averages, and extremes, illness and health). I wish, I hope, I trust – I believe certain tenets, as I understand them, but gathered together, still – in great fatigue, but without so much angst – a surmise – accepting that there are many faces of God, and many paths unto Him. "Great," could be only an anemic "standing in awe."

The feast is in, true, real and true; but the table will empty, to fill again – but not just so, as before.

As a very young woman, I was once asked by my therapist what I would most wish for from life; my reply was honest and straightforward: "… not that much – just everything." My dreams, my sweet dreams, too ephemeral to hold, too distant, now, to grieve: the impossible should not have been conjured into truth, or a form or variety, a mask of truth. The disc – of strength, beauty, grace – purposed will – far, far into – finds descent, and quiet still. Dreams are celestial guideposts which are the impetus for a most good, but the dream is not permanence – not as conceived, originally – long metamorphosing, but ultimately, the dream is refashioned; the question rests on the emphasis factor: the moment, later, time passing, past, forward – eternis.

The tortuous vacillations which comprise the mourning, beside praise – and with its many worded appointments of beauty, this work, "We Lesser Gods," is an open entry to those most true, most troubling feelings of the full adventure of life. We know much, and feel more; remaining is the acceptance most comfortable, provided by secular and spiritual recordings, against the background of all of our lives, formerly and presently; we wish and we grieve; we ponder and fear; all left is the acceptance of what history there is, inside our heart's intuiting sentiments. Perhaps more or less angst will bide, but as "lesser gods" there can reign an affinity which may or may not be recorded, allowing Samaritan givings. We have all of ourselves that we can believe; all of the strength given, and its joys, wounds, and the final taking – all of it all – individual acceptance – finally, without dissonance, angst – surmise.

Elizabeth
October 13, 2015
Nearly midnight

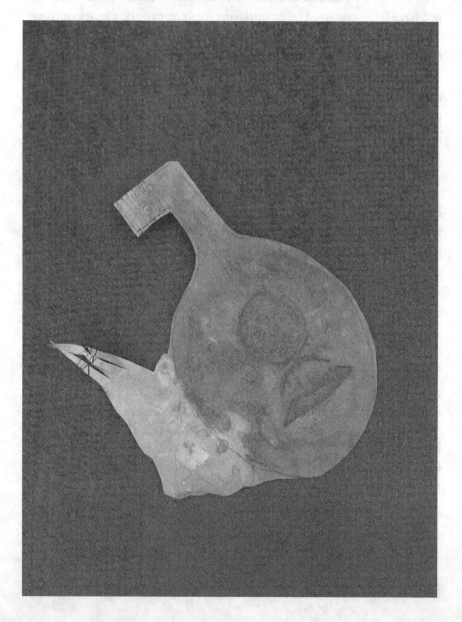

Morning Notes
One, 2015

Gold -- the complete fulfillment --
of tender grass, and its many interwoven
turns, casual, erotic entanglements -- these
beside the peaceful content of
that complication of
beauty and good --
not to so much as to attend,
as to approve --

Wrapped, dressed with iridescent stones,
within wheels groomed of fantasy's chariots,
sumptuously
filled with dreams and the strength they
espouse: let this image drawn above all
seasonal coverings, shadowed -- sunlit and
moonglow -- leave they be -- beyond all time of
countings -- that the joy of the lovely lie in a holy
communion of good,
so documented, the very essence of the word "love,"
heavenly, omnisciently
draped and flowing.

Elizabeth
in deepest night
March, 2015, final week

-- written in intermittent wakings, my thought does not
stray, but is in my vigil of beauty -- sustenance, to my soul --

Morning Notes
Two, 2015

How glorious the lines of the
encaptured, circled matin
movement, in its awareness-- a grace
surmounting extant circumstance --

How the revealing, as its gold becomes,
drawing the gift of day,
the boon of the renaissance of
waiting existentials: these as cognizance
of the crumb to the
foraging cur -- sunrise is!

Elizabeth
March 24, 2015
early morning

-- watching the sun rise, into day -- not so
much on the reality of the foolish, but
simply those sensing, accepting another sitting at the table,
if for only small portions of the feast --

Ribbon Strength

With satin regularity, knotted or teased; rosets or streaming --
ribbons are like relationships
-- if enough binding
once was -- our days, years, experiences, information -- when
they come together, again -- no matter the time, behaviors;
words not spoken,
touches not embraced;
time, yet, with smallest sentiment, pronounces its
extraordinaire bond of adhesive quality whose touching,
acknowledging, remembering, giving
what can be given, as receiving -- becomes;
with these, occurs therein, a kind of
celestial osmosis, and all is as ever was -- a radiant
jewel of familiarity by a drought of
forgetfulness -- instantly, known, but not made conscious -- a jewel is
come -- surly as the "eye of heaven" --
and it, at its most piercing moments --
and though it be noontime, we are left the softly falling
afternoon.

Elizabeth
Christmas Day, 2015 about eleven o'clock am
-- thoughts of our family, as it is today --

Dream Psalm

Let me lie softly, lightly, upon dusty rose and
lavender, complimenting faded scarlet,
that my thoughts lift into the darkness
to fellowship with old dreams
and memories, together with the
expectation we feel of angels, close – over
our engaging and exciting glimpses which
charm our silent, intimate moments.
Let beautylove, touched gently by the a periphery of
longing, fill my heart with pleasantries
too beautiful to know, kept alone
with their distant intimations.
And let me not know the yearning, in reality
offering reflection, of once melodies
of colorful movement, to find forgotten loss, brought again,
of dramatic, illusive grails, those grande and less,
each fair, and with other comely particulars – these
too removed to clasp, left unexamined,
past, too many hours to restore.
And let me not, the flame of, my pining for,
my lovely images, about, declare a stillness in all others;
for I wish to keep them, all, vestiges, and whole, that
I live in the joy of my
salvation – Thy handmaiden, but student of
psalms echoing the glory of
relationship and its joy so promised.

Elizabeth
first week of October, 2014
deep wishes in deepest night

Small Prayer, at Bedtime

-- the flowering closing, beautifully
spent through the early
warmth of day --
I have stepped beside the movements,
within them,
as their first radiance was born.
wonderful, the life of beauty, for it portends
of good;
and if this be my day of debuting white,
or lightly blown neutral of the
concluding shroud --
I die to Thee, contentedly, in praise,
thanksgiving, and petition of
continuing peace.

Elizabeth

small prayer at bedtime
two o'clock am
April 12, 2015

Waiting Glory

A full flowing of beauty came at the
earliest entrance of light;
like a queen descending, to be seated
in her waiting glory,
the day of resurrection began.
Hours processed, moments knew small
splendors, and at beautiful
parameters, the magnificence of spring
was come.
Time, gracious, exacted all that was,
and as the afternoon grew,
reflection, courting the gradually concluding
sunlight, began the feast to come again.
And finishing twilight blessed the
venture,
the day whose bright is commanded by
Dante's stars, God's presence, His warming
love shown to grace us all.

Elizabeth
closing Easter Day, 2014

– the verse covering the anguish drawing a wish
that should have been –

the reference to Dante is from *The Divine Comedy, part, the Inferno* –
"stars" appear throughout his work, indicating the
the warmth in God's love – a lovely metaphor –

a true knowing of the passing of time, prompting a verse –

Veiling Bubbles

Star-kissed bubbles in effervescent spirit have lifted
with an innocent expectation, from earthened
browntones into ochered, favoring
into examination of the towardward;
they have nourished me, led me with wide
softness, through thoughts of the strange and familiar,
from the raven into the silver of my life;
in morning's sparkling pastures into a time of
quickly gleaming sunlight,
and quickly, around the dark; light has processed --
sunlit day – and filled my reservoire of
memorable passings of time until
morning's leften hours.
Peace, unless in unusual discovery, an illusion,
can become true, banishing,
often, concrete, mundane realities,
and gives over to farewelling, white – cold,
into the gentle knowing of falling
rain, warm, and anticipated green.
Then, now, in these days, it may be that in hope is the
movement to our wills, from conclusion
and the self, for in us are the veins, such as those, in palest blue, of
the Madonna's breasts, fair, to, in sympathy,
fashion us, expecting of good,
and lined of sweet – for in this source be acceptance,
and content of mind; in them stand
knowings that lean into the
eternal.

With both hope and an angst, I looked full into the
balcony's glass, to see its affording of a greeting (tall
and very meager) black – rising in an arranging
in the small light, gathering
behind – behind in its upward movement of the
sun.
They had, again, come in, to a communion, almost
immediately, an awareness of our familiar terrestrial.
–Ah, we cannot know, in reality, until the
afternoon, just how much the feast
has set out for us.

Elizabeth
near morning's six o'clock, 2015

my references to the blue veins of the Madonna's breasts can be found
in the several suggestions of R. Browning's work
(one of the two major Victorian British poets),
the verse above, especially, "The Bishop
Orders His Tomb." The color, the image,
and the reality it brings to the
inward eye indicate the care of the holy by
the holy -- in life, in death --
(the Pieta)

Into the Morrow

I will laugh into the morrow,
its now darkness into early morning's bright;
and there, in pleasant dalliance, review my
oil and meal, all in continuous
giving.
I will stand, a matron queen, in robes
of golden wovens,
and let my eyes find light in sunbeams,
my cheek caressed by passing winds
of gentle breath.
And in the morrow, I will wander, to internalize
ancients' postulates, but most, consider the all
of my days, as they settle down
into my truest self.
How does one bide with conclusion and loss,
and honor placed, in the histoire of
all, in lesser portions –
she lives freely in the hope in tomorrow,
and once within it, gathers the laurel, beside
the vinegar and thorns.

Elizabeth
September 4-5, 2014
writing intermittently through the night, having begun a
new Bipolar mood stabilizer medication –
embracing the forward appendage of thought – hope

Is not eternity, in fullest awareness possible, an extended
tomorrow, without fences and seasons –
(place and time)

Evening with the Sky Gods

The winds outside, tonight, suggest the
wandering of the sky gods, in sport, with
that celestial, inside darkness;
insects, with their continuous cadences fall,
gracefully, like dark, golden brocade around the
seams of the gods' robes, as they dance to
nocturnal music.
These beauty, entering out my thought, caught inside
my lighted, familiar rooms,
echo the joy of loveliness, with power and happy presence, a very
issuing need out my soul.
The day had been difficult in that my spirit could find no
peacefulness and light, together, into dusting dreams –
only constant September and its backward
glance to summer's radiance, a longing ever
present, yet when we are imbibing, freely.
Time is a heavy taskmaster, for it remembers as
well as seeing to the forward; that lost
cannot be brought again, just so,
except, if, perhaps, memory of yesterday,
and sentiments rise out their rest to cognitions
of past beauty – its glory, its majesty – most often, event
and instance, to hold until recapture – these are, then,
quite flown away into the beyond.
Andso, sky gods, with robes of glowing moonlight,
among garlands of laughing stars, and dances that step
between planets, graciously garnish my rooms,
lighted and familiar, settled into the night.

Elizabeth
waking to the wind
September 26, 2014

Prayer

HolyfatherGod,
Thou whose Person I have known, always,
yet cannot bide myself enough in Thee –
take my heart, its paltry whole,
only small givings to Thee;
let its povertys be entrances,
arched and blessed, into the presence of Thy grace.
Give comfort when none can be,
And give hope as a purest light;
Give redemption to Thy porcelain doll
in whose hands I have always been kept.
But in emptiness of love and charity have I wandered,
of my own complexities, my need for reason in
matters of faith which had not grown,
as the impoverished seed.
Forgive and accept Thy prodigal who has been lost
to Baels and reinforcers who I thought
more favored my own being in the moment.

Elizabeth
in deepest night
September 22, 2014

Loss

A great many losses can appear, and all loss,
then, can appear in every milieu, for
generalization is a basic learning concept,
from childhood, forward.
Waking, in a very early rising, of which I did
not note the time, I slept, again,
necessitating restoring as to time, place and person –
a proper in establishing well thought; I was able
to identify inconsistencies, and righted my steps,
but with each step echoed the question, "Why."
Brambled knots form in troubled thoughts,
and my surmise which arrived is
that nothing, now, for me, has properties for
me, with which to establish time,
color or any one entity. It bears for an emptiness,
unmeasurable, and the joy of the
once known feast – passed.
Just how we come to this unexplainable circumstance is similar,
probably, to the death of will, what must become the
final altercation of the two absolutes, will and circumstance;
the will becomes outdistanced by particulars combining
in our lives, leaving a brambled knot of the
complete, but it finds a faint memory of
time, one of joy, peace – peace that has existed
before, graciously, to come, again.

Elizabeth
November 3, 2014

the idea present in this verse is one taken from
(William Wordsworth, "Intimations on Immortality")
"We come from God, and we return to God"

Quiet, Still of Thought

The world is mine, when night is secure,
when light, movement --
come -- the quiet still of my thought,
and steps, to, now, the fore.
There is nothing I cannot effect, inside this
ambiance, under the smile, surly of the happy Pleiades,
and on prancing, roan stallion's air, in;
from sentiment and thought,
new dreams come, and
they wander, with purpose,
fragrances from summer warmth, to marry
together all yesterdays' and tomorrows'
knowings,
and our heart, found weary in the struggle of Turnus,
comes to rest the sage's
questionings.
Beauty lays out her fair linen in the
absence of light, and
beside our knowings, beside our quieted struggle,
we pass over, with eager fatigue -- over into the come
faeryland,
it of forgotten, and newly found dreams --
these like marvelously dressed carriages transporting
those lovely to that lovely --
these our forgotten dreams -- supplanting, igniting,
together their full legacy, those
to become, again, new, and more.

Elizabeth
August 1, 2015

Much of my darkness rises out dreams with which
I so much spend energies -- beautiful thought and feelings --
now past the mark
of realization;
yet -- and yet -- perhaps some dreams are
meant to evolve and change -- to better become the
soul of which even I could not have thought,
or known, their wonder.

Elizabeth Afterthought

Messages

Tiger tiger, little lamb --
with a fierce tenderness thou
hadst helped bring me through the fire,
and with patience, and under care, thy
wisdom has provided sentiments to keep
that which houses the lovely and good,
beside hurting calluses that established perseverance through all
wanderings in the wilderness, to find, safe and whole.
Strength has been given through beauty, and
the annals of wounded thought, provided
by a flow of love, and utmost care
of a benevolent Master -- from within my heart
movement of love toward the sounds of generous grace.
Thy imaged messages, thy responses, in sweet, unheard words,
imbue me, and hold me close to the love of good, the
thought of true, the hope in faith --
Thy innocence pours out love over me, that I, as the
instructed child, be made
wealthy in holy wisdom,
altogether safe, and content.

Elizabeth
early morning, July 21, 2015

images from my studies, and lectures, later
(professionally), coming to me upon
waking: William Blake, a favorite imagist and his
famous, small verses -- "Tiger, Tiger, burning bright..." and
"Little Lamb, who made thee..." -- these verses
brought thoughts of this gentle, at times
emotionally ill, English, early Romantic
poet, who worked with grave
intensity at establishing an acceptable, to him, relationship to his God;
his engravings survive, also, and are remarkable
efforts in this life-long endeavor --

-- initiating many warm, positive feelings --

Monarch Moments

In winter's chill, and about, more, cold rain,
blossoms can be purchased from far away climes
which know, everyday, summer's
bright;
and in thoughtfully tender moments, melodies
can sound, intensifying
sentiment, the mourning dove's last lament
of the Southern summer's day.
Yet, creekside Honeysuckle of the Rose's
hue, of Pater's thoughtfulness, and the
green flame of Bamboo, in very freedom –
these are gifts which can come, in especially
lovely, noble moments – of those, true, fraternal and familial.
Ah, the moment – brief, unexpected, at times, first, a
circumstance adversarial, curious, critical – or beginning
can become the splendid reality of the Lily's
rarest, purest smile.
And then, we are content until reflection calls out
our attention, and we wander into the past,
often darkly; into tomorrow, with the gift of anticipation,
and the scourge of angst.
Our thought is a cosem of paradoxical valences, to be
a struggle for a peaceful constancy: we love, and we
will lose; we create, to be masters for a brief day;
we accumulate to give away, and
we live, to die.

That we continue past noonday is a remarkable feat,
but then, the moment is its own "reason to be."
– beautiful and intense, potentially good with understanding –
as stars appear to move and twinkle, in our
approaching their countenance – then, we gather an
intensity of a felt array of sentiments which are rare, if humble –
a foreshadowing of the glory to come
to us, at the close.

Elizabeth
July 8, 2014
ten-thirty pm

images, and the company of moments, insistent,
beautiful and constant in reflection –
Stars always appear in Dante's work when God is especially close in love,
emerging from hell, part The Inferno, The Divine Comedy

Rediscovered "Nice" Lines

spontaneous fragment
at twilight, March 17, 2012

Only "acceptance" is full, if, yet, in emptiness,
and brings enough, even beside our dreams.

In haloed moments, when pleasantries fall about
like luted pastoral scenes, to face futile
unknowing is only a cloud
that passes between us and the warmth
in sunlight, a coming aperitif to
a sweetest cordial, of standing, full being inside small belief.

Silent rose of Rose, leaping emeraled Bamboo;
fullest skies draped of constant
ivory – these hushed into our personal
solitude –
thought in this company offers a repast to
unmeasurable hunger.

Elizabeth
transcribed Mach 11, 2014

We House Karls, All

The hours of he, alone, make wonderful
silence, a day's complete,
the arms of bliss,
the kiss of passion, departed --
all now past as the echos of night call and marry
with the dew fall,
to lift as the meadow's coverlet -- to become again, first,
new arriving hours.
Complextion is all in the nausea of illness
or wellness of the heart, and we embrace the bliss
or kiss, just so --
Oh Holyfathergod, let the purest raiment of
angelic white, the streaming blood, wetted scarlet, of martyrs'
corporal being, the lap of endurance, worn
into sweetened soil, as the child yet sleeps --
if, please, these images be our rainbow, as dusk, with stars
drink into the away our fatigue, to fill,
again, with holy breath, the quiet not ever, yet asked, but let be kept,
already given.
Dusk and silence, solitude -- praise of the drama of the noble
house in which we each, all do bide -- let these
surround the wonderment of life,
the kingly soul, to protect, to defend, to die --
in the quiet for the preservation of truth. The house
karl, we all to be, who carries the only,
ever significance: the labor of everyman is his day -- grace
into redemption, salvation, our all of good.

-- bejeweled fabrics, of clothiers, fine, tassels, fringe --
muscles, smooth, firm, intractable; golden notions, wide of
fullest breath; eyes whose stars, center clear; and neighs of triumph to
everyman, his own to reign into fullest glory, supporting, below --.
and let us to know, finally, that words, well-chosen, masterly stitched
vestments, and silver, in its new light -- these are merely our
humble symbols of that we feel, the sentiment
true, the image, crafted --
allow the image not to come to dress the sentiment into
pitiable piety.

Elizabeth
July 12, 2015, transcription:
having been scripted several days earlier
-- I cannot remember the occasion of the writing of
this verse, only it being in the deep of night --
inner voices to my conscious reason, from
stimuli within the finished day --

Small, Holy Conversation

If in the grande smallness of this
beautiful room,
my thoughtful cathedral –
if I offer a wishful, humble petition
to Thy hearing, biding –
if – I shall:
a carriage of solitude,
passing upward, carrying great
thanksgivings, with
my penitent amen:
Lord have mercy, Lord have mercy,
Lord have mercy.

Elizabeth
in deepest night (one-forty am)
January 18, 2015

from a Russian Orthodox prayer,
taught to me in difficult times by Father Paul Yerger,
Clinton, Mississippi – 1995 – 2000, following –

Let the gentle whisperings of the dark, the closing,
hoarse outings of my south woods' geese,
and the sometimes angstful, yet
reflecting gratefulness, in thought – together with the bold approach
to giving strength –
let this conversation of seeking thoughts
arrange in acceptable offerings.

Sabbath Feast

In thought, and visual wanderings,
I survey wealth caught into the new day;
with all gratefulness, I intuit, yet
truly know,
that I have lived, all of my life, for this only
moment –
it to be repeated, no matter the circumstance
or posture of "dingas" –
I am grateful for generous benevolence that
allows me to come to table of the feast – in every
frame of thought, every image found through
my senses.
It is Sabbath, and the glory of summer sunlight
is touching all of terrestrial holdings: increasing blue
sky, leaves, an emerald sculpting of very
grace;
flowers, with the added appointment of
fragrance, like moving dancers, in color, to the
music of a celestial narrative –
yet a blessed quiet, the husbandman of
present peace.
Sunday morning – early – God, ever, now, and
shepherd throughout eternity – as surely
as the moor, as surely as the sea –
the chart, already given.

Elizabeth
early Sunday morning, about eight o'clock
July 6, 2014
greatly aware, and more greatly, appreciative

– the two poets referenced above are Rilke, the
very fine, (and, now, most exalted,
possibly) German poet ("dingas" – "things")
and Ms. Emily Dickinson, the early
American imagist ("I Never Saw a Moor") –

First Conceived to be

*The becoming flesh tones of the early
morning's first Rose; and the fragrant dust
effervescing out the Southern Lily's golden throat --
these the beginning good as good can conceived to be:
-- given out the dark of night's
alone, unattended separation into the sunlit
glory of new morning:
first voice of breath --
and in arriving hours as we come to lie down in
humble gratitude,
at the dying of quietening light,
remember to us the hue of the Rose, the dust of the
Lily --
as rarities from ancient crusades, intense with
powers that brought them present:
this power watch over our dark unknowings,
and rise us to our gifts that will eagerly offer the quest of
coming day.*

Elizabeth
October 4, 2015
*about twelve- fifteen, not being able to get off to sleep; Holy Presence
let my pen guide my thought into a brief repose --*

*the phenomenon of life: rise to effort -- struggle into pause -- beauty,
falling sun stars until twilight sparklings
illuminate the dark -- ah, "the way of all flesh..." Somerset Maugham*

Their Peace

In a moment of sudden awareness,
I knew a complete silence:
the fresh bouquet only breathed its beauty
to me;
the heavy, full darkness, outdoors,
only stood by in silent patience;
and in myself I felt only a quietness and
stillness,
a complete acceptance of
the song of night.
In this procession, a widening of perceptual
energies felt movement, for I knew the sounds of
distant, barking dogs – spontaneous,
comfortable, warm, across the cold
of winter,
in the joy of their being.
New maneuvers of my thought quickly expressed,
and I thought – is this a quietness, most, within myself;
is there no word, no voice – no telling of
the joy in being –
pain, loss, grey, winter – with these, in the weighing, am
I found subordinate to distant, barking dogs –
Quickly, I reached for my pen, with immediacy,
purpose – their peace, joyfully sounding.

Elizabeth
in deepest night
January 12, 2014

Daddy heard dogs barking in the night.

A Formed Magnificat

Having just, earlier, placed a Gardenia
blossom under the edge of my pillow, its
valour white, failing, but gathering more sweetness, as it ecrues –
in this moment, a sudden awareness filled my thought,
that I was, in some form of presence,
aware of my mother and father – either alone of them, or
they, one without the other, yet we, somehow, in an
omniscient knowing Ivory white into ecru shadowing,
faces, then, as at the last, now bronzed, and glowing,
but in difficulty without a companion –
– oh, day, the measure of life we all can claim
until it is taken – what significance brings these images:
can they be deciphered -- messages from warm
constellations inside my heart –
is all of true beauty lost to
time, in denial and confusion; does thought become
turbulent, with pawns, knights, bishops and kings
about, quietening mature procession.
If constancy not be our bulwark, our climes advance,
full, with the persecution of the rack – only, now, of
sounding staccatos and darkened dirges – of woes and waves;
color incompatible, edicts and writs, unconscionable.
Fragrance, sweet of childhood lore, and faces bronzed, glowing,
do not leave me in confusion, if in protective guise –
for thou art my "rock," the strength of the arm of the sling,
my "cattle upon a thousand hills."
Add mercy, now, to instruction: gift an added day of first
ivory fragrance, bronzed lips to touch,
clasped, bronze hands, these together.

Elizabeth
June 18-19, 2014
early evening, six-thirty pm
– poignant sentiment, growing from images, strong, flowing, each
from out the other – celebrated in my heart – a formed magnificat;
the Gardenia blossom, in my verse, is from a plant of many blossoms,
rooted by my father's hand, from his and my mother's
garden, before their deaths –

a dream, out images, all, from long ago, and
far away – and not with despair,
but bringing content –

the words "rock," "strength of the arm,"
and "cattle" can be referenced
back to Holy Scripture, the recorded, one Christian God –

"Stuff"

-- sound, out silence which had kept
the night:
waking stuff, partial awareness,
rather than immediate,
whole knowing stuff --
dream stuff -- images passing quickly,
understandings fragmenting into the whole,
familiar stuff;
knowings out intermittent awareness --
stuff of confusion, into sentiment
stuff --
a butterfly of idea flitted by -- come from all
of where, full of every, to be
alive ever: colorings of a former
spring, and I knew the day, the season,
my self, my own stuff --
Palm Sunday, lunar anniversary, green before scarlet,
and a finishing quiet before birth:
careful, precious stuff --
man, provision -- acceptance -- redemption:
feast stuff, once again, having been
shadowed a small season;
emergent, coming victorious --

Elizabeth
just at first light
March 29, 2015

feeling well, almost "burdened" with gratitude:
not to "go gently into that
sweet night...."

the partial quote, above, is from the verse of twentieth
century, American poet, Dylan Thomas: "Let
me not go gentle into that sweet Night;"

-- the reference to "lunar anniversary"
reminds again, after all of the years,
the Sunday in Easter, at Jimmy's home, with his parents and family,
my sudden "break," and the poignant saga which unfolded
into today -- I am, yet, sorry, so sorry, but
grateful for the beauty such has
provided --

Mine, of the South Woods

The geese, which nest in my South woods –
to fly out at dew fall, and into, again, at dusk –
are, in these moments, silent.
And yet, I know they are present, as
the close familiar; I love them, in their soundings,
as would I, a sweet memory,
for they do not wound, or forget, and in these
principles of behavior, I gather them to me.
My geese, these if my South woods,
whose saga I have written in earlier days,
have become, in their soundings,
and in their silences, my friends,
almost as a natural occurrence – almost as a
good – truly, as a good –
constant, and in their genetic holdings, as kind as the
Natural is, but by attention to schedule and
senses, beauty expectancy, a variety of order
which rolls out a lovely path in
the troubled frenzy of the every day –
Into the night they sing, with smaller sounds into
the fuller dark: a proposal of peace,
a doing of good, and, with these, a natural flock,
I am content.

– not carat, or rhine nor sandgrain or wind,
more, movement in the heart –
such, must, to still, but joyful that
it can be, and so accounted –

Elizabeth
at dusk, February 18, 2014
with David and John in the afternoon –
family and friend – gifts of great love, close, now,
inside my heart – so good is God –

Another Tasting
(a morning verse)

In the day's close becoming,
settled into quiet,
the shadow to its self beside,
with an ease, and with a joy,
the wait of faith comes to sit with me.
Much was, and much is, of blackberries and
rainshowers,
those of summer's reprieve, still, to the spirit.
Oh, heavy chest of thought, let your
bramble untwine, gently, to
bind about my heart,
that my wait in this early morning
be my complete in sense and thought.

Oh now, now, the spring of beauty, of beauty
in opening day;
the splendor, the vine in harvest, first, the
reality of truth;
the acuity of long sought wisdom, and the
coming together of every atom, every cell -- every amen --
each heartbeat in the promise of
another,
of that tasted fully, before.

Elizabeth
-- on waking in another, summer's early quietening;
sweet sting of sorrow, but joy accepted,
as I catch the baton --
August 16, 2015

I often reach back for the symbol/image of
the baton to be caught from another,
fondly remembering my eldest brother reaching during the mile
relay track event in high school, Clinton,
Ms. Such was his motivation,
always, even in the most adverse of circumstance;
the image will always be with me,
as its poignant meaning.

September Evening

The evening is come, a September
evening,
in the gloaming when secrets crowd
with their recognized presence.
I wish me my steps, easily, my hope not in
twilight,
nor my apples from the feast cast about
as nightingale's roses,
for I have no love, only that of the first gift,
of the blessing of breath,
the awareness of self and where all places
arrange.
Let me know more than is left of the day –
review – yes – but not conclusion;
quiet my restlessness with the warmth of
yesterday,
and the promises of, yet, another
tomorrow.
Let my hand hold in the truth of good,
the strength in faith, with
peace of the house – all gathered in,
the blessing having been sung.

Elizabeth
seven-fifteen pm
early dark, with rain
first week of September, 2014

In Absence

When no priest is to our comfort,
an emptiness, clouded of storms, turns, and
with great fatigue -- such like blows, into a malestrum --
its verities lacking -- this darkness, deep into our hearts;
the natural dancing of flowers in bouquets
forget their alter beauty, moving shapes, and
despite holding, still, present colors;
graceful winds no longer lift, in spritely fashion,
our steps,
for the priest hears our voices, augmenting our steps, passing --
to enter them into Presence, that a hearing is
given, allowing forgiveness and redemption.
When we find, in this alone, that we are a
bark, more than one adrift, but one, without help -- not --
solitude,
then, can become unable to work its medicinal comforting and
cleansing, leaving us to the most grievous struggle --
(when a priest is required) --
that of searching, to find in this great deprivation,
a need of filling
a portion of tainted self, the prodigal,
in the shadow of Eden.

Elizabeth
July 15-16, 2015

-- the brotherhood of man is, in a fashion,
en mass, a priest at hand, as is
a complete seeking a oneness with the Grande Natural --
individuation often brings stain, and oneness with "the face of God,"
(C. Kingsley) can help with the process of redeeming -- as, more, the
coming together in truth (confession) with a brother --

a note of appreciation of the relationship, of a oneness in spirit with my
physician and brother, seen today, in session -- at noontime --
July 16, 2015

Placed Deference

Why to reach to gather the flower,
to offer it first deference
before bowing in prayerful, holy
conversation.
Of celestial's spiritual courtesy,
the flower is eternal, its cycles in great, and
sensitive strength,
coming to us again, and again, ages into eons.
It is fresh of any of that unclean; it is beautiful,
a fairness flawless, and in its purity a
vessel holding the very presence
of God.
Representation in this fashion is instruction exemplaraire.
-- no works are required, but to be --
and when we are in place to know this
beatitude, we, then, bow before clasping,
acknowledging the Presence of
the many faces of God -- close, familiar, intimate:
Holy Presence -- now -- then -- all of ever.

Elizabeth
Saturday, April 11, 2015
-- in early afternoon beauty, its joy to hold, yet,
in quiet reflection of all natural beauty, in springtime's round --
"I am That I am."
-- Holy Scripture --

Keep Us, Still

A fire, in raging, scarlet grande --
or the diminutive, struggling in pressured throws;
volcanoes rumbling with fierce heat and
pressed togetherness;
the once formidable train, "the iron horse,"
passing off with a gust of billowing heat and
steam of white and grey:
amazing heaviness in swiftness, and then, the
snows of Garmish, to offer angelic, soft winds of blowing white,
an ephemeral covering, quickly passing.
Ah, Holyfathergod -- at the closing of the day,
let us fall in gratitude for the small, soft peace in our hearts:
for the grace of the silent rhapsody of an
opening flower; the contentedly grazing cattle; the
infant asleep in its security of love.
We cannot return to simplicity, but grant, please, yes, please -- anoint our
spirits with its beauty.

Elizabeth
just at bedtime
September 13, 2015
a beautiful Sabbath

"As Good"

Easy comes, the way of the moment --
all colorings, soundings -- movements --
full reality becomes, is -- of the awareness we
suddenly and reluctantly, if with
satisfaction, follow the waking into, almost as if now
metamorphosed into a planned, if small eternity -- one
which somehow rests in expected place, as if following preludes,
propers, charms -- and halos lighted, with descriptive directives
to become officer to spontaneous responses, having
always been in vintage royalty, of highborn lineage, ever,
and with septres and crowns beside.
-- very being, and in its full recognition, is, if quickly passing,
eventually classic hedonia, the pleasure
giving impetus to movement, together with competition,
birthing critical observation, and, often, unwise conclusion --
bold, we become, in trysts with these small
recognitions -- even yet, to find ourselves
upon the wall, tenuously, in suggestion of the
egg's fall.

The matter of insight and knowing is a coin (it coming of reason)
of rare complexion, lighted and shadowed by its
companion self, sentiment;
these, comprised the universal stage, underscoring
one of the early twentieth century, Russian author's
conclusions: no matter the tense of awareness -- then, now, ever --
man, because of his infrequent exchanges with the commodity of
awareness -- fares poorly more often than could be wished:
we are not as good as we know how to be
("The Father" A. Chekhov).

Those variables which contribute to the "good aware" need be
acceptance when recognized (out whatever fashion), loved
and utilized in daily portions. Then -- if we can
not always be "as good as we know how to
be" -- perhaps the mark might be
to make effort, to approach "as good as we know...."

Elizabeth
-- just at midnight, Good Friday of another Holy Week, passed --
a beautiful day of gratitude and praise
April 3-4, 2015
-- Richard's seventy-second birthday --

Inward Eye

(softest, safest cub)

It is in now that night
is wandering,
to find a blanketed nest --
throughout the shadows, their dimming objects,
but, more, into the reality in which
I find my struggle --
night-time walks the difficult road
of truth -- no sound, bells silent, no touch, my company
unfashionable these recent seasons,
and from the long way back,
"gatherings in" were foremost, a time of thought,
peace, and reflection, of dreams and small
chores left from the day, these allowing small
pleasantries, and contained angst to the
side.
Night does not see, of lighted wet, but permits
unfolding scenes from the internal eye,
and this window opens into our very hearts;
Oh night, rest our being and soothe our spirits,
most in the furor of which we cannot
see particulars that threaten -- oh Night, be kind.

Elizabeth
thoughts on passing into sleep
August 5, 2015

-- tired, the usual sad, weary, but of the knowing that the
fierceness in Dam Night is kind to her cubs; they sleep
in softest safety --

Putting Away ...

In the beauty of winter's starlight,
when the self is alone, together, with
thought,
patience works its charm, and warmth knows
the inside seam of being –
joy can smile to pleasurable scenes
which bests the romantic pastoral, to compose
a sonnet, yet, a lovely, flowing nocturne – these of, most,
a peace, inside the closet of simple
pleasures, and, perhaps, some portion
of the psalmist's content,
following the offering up of all a
self can tend.

Elizabeth
January 26, 2014
one-twenty am

a statement to put away with a good day –

In Times

In times when sentiment falls about like the golden
flax that faeries weave,
my dissonance is oppressive, beyond the
voice of life, for many knowings
cover our consciousness -- could be
poor metal with silver, with all of their different
accompaniments, finding reconciliation by the deep,
wide reaching pulsations of kindred hearts.
Perhaps I should have stayed, or if to
leave, to have made a change grande, deep, a traversment
not ever thought, again, to be healed.
And in going, I should not have looked back --
for in such is an Achilles' wound. It may be that had I
stayed, flowers in all their simple, woodland
glory should have been enough, not
requiring climes of different lineage, against the walls
of the cultivated passing of time.
-- but the Poppies -- the worded descriptions,
dressing truths, not truly
foreign to me, but sustenance and evidence to my soul.

Beside my going, drift the faces of my little
"brownskins," in play and finding -- they into a level
more comfortable -- less hurt -- but a delicacy of
homesickness that is made a tolerable one to me --
in the breath and width of understanding -- knowing, feeling --
yet, together, the
many faces, the wealth of the multiple paths to God.
Evaluations are difficult, for reason is like the
stone, and sentiment, the early petal; to marry them into
a good peace is an act of hurting courage, release,
and reconciliation.

Elizabeth
Thanksgiving Eve, 2015

Sentiments at Christmastime

concluding the year
2015
The heart does not forget, but holds, close, its
most beauty;
bound, and gently corded of pouring gold,
the past;
evoking the qualities of invitation and passion of the present,
and
awareness and holding in thought, with jeweled
clasps,
the promised hours of tomorrow.

Elizabeth
December 13, 2015
-- the complete treasure of the day --
after eleven o'clock pm

Dissonance

Dissonance

Deep and Weighted

Deep and weighted, heavily, the
wounds of the heart, those which fall onto
the days of maturity,
that purposed into revealing.
We hold them as we cling to their
executioners,
for they are, in birthing perception,
all the same.
Dependence is an unhappy ingredient
of love, a sweet fragrance
which becomes, on occasions, too frequently,
the vinegar accompanying
fated thorns.

Elizabeth
in deepest night
March 22, 2015

my learning to capture, yet to be raptured:
when reading verses composed five -- six years ago,
written: I see, feel that expressions are from another present,
a residual holding of beauty brought forward from deep love of
the gifts of thought and perceptions --
this construct is unclear, and I hold, as with a seasoned, warrior's
fierceness -- to the moment, to the present, here in the reality of
now, to gather, still, and to add to --

perhaps -- all is, all that ever was, beauty presence being
added into with the continual processing --

How lovely --- how encouraging! a returned
moment of insight with strength --

Unhappy Path

The path of our extended steps becomes -- though
at times of worthy observation --
obscure, deceptive, even obtuse, althewhile
awarding its beauty -- that ledgered, some
of kin, camaraderie
and loves, inside the self, realized --
adding to, holy men and the lowly, faithful
hunt, alongside the Grande Natural.
Users and takers hang about, as does the most low,
the feigned, sincerely good and understanding --
yet, and conclusively,
further, well, for in the duration, intertwined with time,
distance, cultivated words, and
contrived knowings -- in such
arrangements, extended -- they falter, as those often
of my heart, my purse, my gifts -- I would have
willingly exchanged -- allowing the entire
charade continue -- had not such others in their selfish perceptions
of my unknowings -- been foundation, alone, enough,
but by,
inside, my secret, unhappy -- hurting insight of intervention and
intervention, fluid, independent thought.
-- how foolish, contented in their uncertainties, these
fools -- I always knew -- perhaps in the absence of a blossom,
the avoidance of complimenting, forgetting the wallet --
I always knew -- perhaps in the absence of a
blossom, The avoidance of complimenting,
forgetting the wallet -- I always knew, even
if only, most, in the afterward;

but they took, in false assurance; I allowed,
continuing an exchange which, in the full circle may
have added a coin or so to their larder, but added
a wealth in knowing to mine,
to wander, in the universality of thought.
-- how foolish, contented in their uncertainties, these
unknowing -- unknowing, in a bramble of ignorance,
the dark mark of ill will, whatever its origin,
and false confidence resting on the taker's
uncomfortable bed of tainted straw -- these can, only with difficulty
and unmeasured sacrifice, find in one's self the confidence he praises,
the wisdom he cannot learn -- yet, continuously proclaims.
The better is the wisdom found by he,
among infrequent, quiet moments,
to observe, to arrive to smile -- in content (of his unacknowledged
knowings).
-- sad, sad -- the feigned sport -- partial, yet -- search -- already
in the belly of such players' struggle, and defeat -- to be heard, full,
becoming foul, and disposed into the dark--
and so -- but what price glory --

Truth is not, in many wisdoms, static, but found in learning
its standing, changing postulates.
Being willful is not wise; being willful when one
can be so in circumstances which call for its
property of being wise is the tenet of new choice.
We have, now, no such as the care, the need
for crusades, and martyrdom -- or we have deteriorated to the
level of a new martyrdom -- blood and death,
but that, untruly -- surface lights, only.

The Universal Mind does not require our breath
except when our thought fails a final holding of truth.
An evolving of wide circumstances, which renders
Universal Mind (truth) conceptually apart from
former times, finds its historical concept
nearly undefended or supported.

Elizabeth
in deepest night/early day
March 24, 2015

Comment
an Elizabeth afterthought

From the beginning subject of the unfortunate example of the
untruthful partner, in modern dress, though not greatly
different from earlier relationships, a lostness is
experienced -- at the least at some uneasily found level;
Women, of course, have "slips that show," also.

Martyrs, too, have a different description, in more recent
perceptive evaluations. Perhaps the better conclusion is to use
another "more current" attempt at "whole truth:"
We are physical and psychological creatures who are born into
circumstances not our conscious own. We become
who we are by observation, instruction, and

experience, added to the circumstances already
noted. It may be that whether we
become "good "men or women (of truth/
wisdom) with which to struggle, yet to die
physically or spiritually -- we can say we "know," but we cannot say,
without any error, the recipe for each
individual; we would defile "truth" as
we draped robes of honor around it.
Because of the concept of a Spiritual Presence -- from time
of "the first" time, or a great need for such, it remains the
supreme question in life -- home, community,
city, nation -- but, as sad, as sweet --
most individually.
Semantics reign, exist in the world of we "lesser"
gods. However, the question, most weighted,
the question most loving, and hurting -- aware
or no -- can be found only where
it is felt -- all else to the side -- in the heart.

Out My Beggar Soul ...

Out my beggar soul, I cry forth,
against the grey middle,
a very battleground of grasping,
losing hold;
issuance from vials; ponderings; conversations
and prayerful petitions, filled of want –
altogether, these, an indolent weeping.
Give to me, dream to me,
oh, Mountain, scenes of whole excellence,
beauty, and wisdom,
a playfulness out regained innocence,
and a bed of straw on which animals sleep,
unattended, unaware,
in fullest peace.

Elizabeth
early morning, three-fifty-five am
March 8, 2014

– after working through an essay on "the self." for Sarah;
could not find "the feast," this time:
a fragment of a prayer –

the expression of "oh Mountain" is a reference to the ancient
epic *Gilgamesh,* a petition to a spiritual source
for wisdom and truth –

Difficult Moments

Perhaps, perhaps — of the all of it,
we can only live, with any fullness,
our summers: these beautiful
combinations when will and circumstance
embrace the moment, together.
We cannot demand them, or know the particulars
of their coming, other than a dream — like
expectancy, and willingness to accept, understanding
the ephemeral nature of spring, the
certainty of winter.
Our summers come out solitude and effort,
alongside the activity of a togetherness with
others, these stances each creating
an ambiance of warmth, lovely, images, a complexion
of fairest light.
Parameters, around, are always — dark and full of nothingness,
an ennui, pressing the reality of accepting
our summers, on somewise, alone,
these singular phenomena comprising our feasts,
at whose table we sit often, and long.
Like a train moving its image into the distance,
our days gather the light of our, then, frugal summers,
the parameters of winter, grey into an eternity
of surmise.

Elizabeth
Febrary 9, 2015

these moments pulling will from me, following
days and days, difficult, difficult —

New Feast

Darkness behind me,
Light, coyly, but with an innocent good,
before;
a very confusion of stimuli -- both of reason,
and fancy -- touching my thought --
these, all, together billowing
up as smoke from great flames, reaching,
inside me --
this verse, this unrehearsed, spontaneous
sonnet, filled with words unheard -- unwritten by plume,
and left unsounded by spoken voice,
ought the silence of the new day.
My tenuous hold on my burdened will, it
becoming unable to balance and achieve constancy
from which to enter and pursue the
objective cosmos of my own --
I, as one of the affectation of the
quaffing of a medieval spiritual, and physical wine,
found, laying, by my worn, yet, willing heart:
the offering, once again, of the
giving feast.
Samaritans entered, cock-like, but purposely darting
about, like rogues and street ruffians,
bathed and instructed, taking away the incisive, almost
reactive come of memory in its
unmerciful guise, its skillful touch of residual
gratitude.

Left -- found a beautiful wound, whole enough --
no more, its scarlet flowing --
With the fullest light established, the sunrise has became both a
salutation, and a valediction; my place
at table, again, waited, and the path of recent time past
was farewelling.
In awareness, is life -- out whose gift its incestuous
self enjoins with the circumstance
provided; the day is, to be, still, its more.

Elizabeth
March 28, 2015
seven o'clock am

Inside Rooms

When slipping past the finger and tea cup,
past the clock, the calendar, the sun making
its way into the westward dim,
a reality – of fancy, of yesterday – of particular
moments, identifiable by very closed,
intimate symbols –
this reality allows exploration into the depts of self –
of myth, and fable, inside proverbs learned, early,
or through individual steps leaning into
shrouded perceptions.
Perhaps recognizing truth is a fancy, a learned response seen
rehearsed in the metropolitan gardens of life;
perhaps it is the wish fulfillment with
unconscious truisms that are kind to our needs,
alongside a fatigued sparring that lets us
will all others to see the meadows, and alleyways,
the incense-filled and clouded temples, yet the
plains of Carthage, revisited – all as we see – to pass before our
inward eye.
We are charged, then, with the phantom dragon of
doubt, the malignant malaise of hurt and pity, to falter
under our own misinterpretations,
false principles, and, eventually,
estrangement.
There is no antidote to truth, save its accuracy in wholeness,
to, then, in its beauty, find lodging for all
rooms of soul.

Elizabeth
September 7, 2014
allowing my thoughts to wander, my pen its
lieutenant of movement –
at twilight, of my birthday

The Coming of Beauty

Of full beauty, one might conclude
a kind of waiting is included,
a patience of placid, pasteled water, sensing moving,
increasing light --
a quiet anticipation which
erupts into a growing rapture,
a parfumed bouquet -- be the players
individuals, representatives of the grande natural,
yet, a coming of ease in the sweet taking
of thought.
-- reflection, out heavy time, and its enhancing
of judgment allowed, gifts perceptive wings, on which
we process to lingering groves, valleys of secret,
darkness falling onto the constant heath --
memorial, altogether, of a fuller awareness --

Elizabeth
June 25, 2015
transcribed, nine-thirty pm

-- on thoughts of yesterday's session, and the dissonance into
thought it has precipitated --
-- can I bear thee -- Ah, April into September, I into
my own: so many gatherings of the now; where do I rest
myself, and howso, groom into --

Steps

Resolve of Abraham, the faith of Noah;
the inconsistent, generous weakness of Peter, the agony of
unmeasured repentance of Paul -- these, with the
unfulfilled vision of Moses -- narrative, fable, myth -- the
vehicle does not begin the turn --
these strengths were: at sometime, somewhere, if
metamorphosed, in telling,
and re-telling.
Could we not, for our own imaged self, select
some pattern to replace the lost, redeem the fallen;
restore the dissonance -- find strength of the Thou in
heart -- its peace, justice, mercy -- find, restore life more
than the disillusionment of a party, ending with an
emptiness -- only partially remembered --
just enough to try and fill again.

Thought is the working out of the steps of our lives;
we can whistle and amble along; we can work within silent
conversations, and we can play and sing in
worship, but the steps must be taken, finally, to an
accounting.
-- "American Beauty," the ultimate death of the brown
paper bag -- blowing, bouncing about,
of no thought of any symbolism to the aimlessness
of our lives -- to ourselves, and more pronounced,
to others --
To be the "brother mine" is noble when true, but
truths without boundaries become "courtesies,"
then expectations, behaviors
toward allowing license for all.

-- wandering thoughts --
Thou of Thee in me -- pray Thou, Thyself, in me --
Elizabeth
Thoughts...

the line "Pray Thou, Thyself, in me," is from "prayer
cards" gifted of my friend, Janice, in the Russian
Orthodox Church, in Clinton, MS -- years ago

Moment's Complexion

The day is one of stark reality;
the cold of winter, the sun, in its bright,
suggesting its impossible distance --
the sound is that of complete,
without qualities, only silence, so that even the bells
have entered again.
There is only one aspect to this reality that
is more than its constancy -- the
knowing: the moment, glaringly cold, showing
all the passed summer -- and alone -- to silence, with
only the company of my thought.
These qualities fill my moment,
my full reality, for dreams and their expectations
do not flourish in emptiness -- this moment --
hollow conversation, the image of harpies, in reflection;
long, dark and winding hallways: and asides, bitter --
dragons breathing fire without into ash -- the constant
echo of the pounding feet of the hound.
In cerebral absence -- emptiness -- oh moments, do not pass away
without leaving less one gift, a thread of, perhaps, scarlet, a hue
of memory's suggestion, laughter when it was without its
sting -- Holly berries that come to glow, assenting to our smiles.
We do not, often, but we do know, at times
of sweet selection,
our moments, when we are in them, and
when we are in them, alone -- or rare, select -- one of a
treasure, true -- in truth, a grail to pursue --
in a moment of oneness.

Elizabeth
November 24, 2015
-- appraisal --

In Deepest Night, I

Oh Spirit, Thine of time of all Being,
joy, and grief;
in these poorly held, wretched moments,
help me to see the glory of the gift of being.
Hold close to Thy widened breast,
Thy sweetness of care for all,
those with houses, large, and grande, beside
the humble hut of mud and straw.
Let know we all Thy boundless giving,
never forgetting the smallest twig -- that it fell from
heights of most exalted form, from beauty of words
indescribable, to lie a token of Thy
pleasing at beauty spent -- the greatest dialogue which
can be spoken of we, mortals, in any discourse --
the larger purpose of all, the mind
infinite, pure --
the path of the beautiful and good,
its immeasurable wealth of the absolute
burden, exalted -- its larder of truth.

Elizabeth
almost eleven pm
thoughts which bring some calming to my ever dissonance --
June 4, 2015

In Deepest Night, II

-- difficult, difficult to know --
to feel, free, full truth in the face of being;
We, bending of will in its triumphant struggle -- this circumstance of
our days.
Does the real turn in time to a goodness, more a
holiness -- or does the umbered, ochered flesh of earth
fragrance its purpose, to become a lifting, a
billowing up of formless nothing into what we
dreamers once hailed the abundant heavens, above in
majestic blue.
Is so that eternity truly can match the width of thought,
to let it, or not, die it to formlessness --
unknowing, an endless path of quiet for all of eons to retrace
the boundless glory, the depths of less, the climb back to honor
and truth -- all to never be acknowledged or
therever, again, be, casting aside the radiance, the
rapture which shadows, always, the timeless way.

Elizabeth

eleven pm
June 4, 2015

honor, why -- purpose laid out to view -- difficult, difficult --
I am spent...

let darkness balm me, and stillness die my thought with
messages I cannot accept, yet to pull me into their own --

Sweet Repose

And as the soft of love, the sleep of sweet
repose drifted into my rooms,
and settled over me, like the fragranced powder of memory, down,
down -- over the willing old.
It was a journey of hours long -- I knew the strength
taken, when first aware -- lands and paths,
surly as those wandered about by Odysseus;
but I did not live them, knowingly,
not in my dreams of much conquer, but in
gentlest rest while requiring:
the moment when towers are felled, walls broken through -- small
smoke, of only greyvine coloring, lifting
into the above, into the vastly sweetness of peace.
These moments of redemption blessed my soul,
and for the length that grace decides, I awakened to new day --
...spent, yet again given over to steps whose fatigue had been quieted,
my piercings, my bursted wounds soothed,
anointed -- my blood now staid --
poured over by Samaritan balms --
place to me, in this time, only, the disc -- for
I am, again, ready -- to turn, poised
to round, and, with perfect bent, to let it up, into graceful movement,
into the away, and its quiet descent.

Elizabeth
-- on waking, from a night which I know only
in sentiment: joyfully awake, presently --
June 16, 2015
seven o' clock am

Fullest Intention

The difficulties of the odyssey of life
encompass, encourage disillusionment --
if not for the reprieve of beauty --
and beauty embraces many components;
if we faint, we rise -- if we weep, we rearrange:
there is endless resilience in all our hearts, if not absolute
wonder, that we continue without ultimately faltering --
often, most recognizing with strength and with will.
Somewhere in our closeted spirit, the becoming evening star,
and the rising sun -- their faces in castings show the
fraternity, the love
that being can know.
The earth sustains, and when the sky calls and sings,
we survive --
until we give back to the gift that was benevolent
grace extended to us; what happens to
the wrapping does not matter --
the wager, the exchange was the intent of the turn.

Elizabeth
first week of November, 2015

Monarch Moments

In winter's chill, and about, more, cold rain,
blossoms can be purchased from far away climes
which know, everyday, summer's
bright;
and in thoughtfully tender moments, melodies
can sound, intensifying
sentiment, the mourning dove's last lament
of the Southern summer's day.
Yet, creekside Honeysuckle of the Rose's
hue, of Pater's thoughtfulness, and the
green flame of Bamboo, in very freedom –
these are gifts which can come, in especially
lovely, noble moments – of those, true, fraternal and familial.
Ah, the moment – brief, unexpected, at times, first, a
circumstance adversarial, curious, critical – or beginning
can become the splendid reality of the Lily's
rarest, purest smile.
And then, we are content until reflection calls out
our attention, and we wander into the past,
often darkly; into tomorrow, with the gift of anticipation,
and the scourge of angst.
Our thought is a cosem of paradoxical valences, to be
a struggle for a peaceful constancy: we love, and we
will lose; we create, to be masters for a brief day;
we accumulate to give away, and
we live, to die.

That we continue past noonday is a remarkable feat,
but then, the moment is its own "reason to be."
– beautiful and intense, potentially good with understanding –
as stars appear to move and twinkle, in our
approaching their countenance – then, we gather an
intensity of a felt array of sentiments which are rare, if humble –
a foreshadowing of the glory to come
to us, at the close.

Elizabeth
July 8, 2014
ten-thirty pm

images, and the company of moments, insistent,
beautiful and constant in reflection –
Stars always appear in Dante's work when God is especially close in love,
emerging from hell, part The Inferno, The Divine Comedy

Poem

The beauty of any one entity perceived
is not in its physical qualities, its objective
efforts toward reality –
but holds in the dressings we, the observers, the
giving and receiving participants, establish,
in the exchange of the prescribed interaction.
The established time, in company or solidarity,
the call to our senses – in oneness or together –
and these combined, impact – gentle and
easily received – or with more
strength and complexity – yet – these, each call to our
truly fragile "self," in the moment, selectively –
these small, or so appearing,
making absolute, the experience –
as inside, light flashing, wind in movement,
so, by the gods, themselves,
or the tremulously striking of a final blow,
more, a touch, to the heart –
in this fashion is significance drawn:
joy or grief, loss or keeping – the very suggestion that
we are – indeed –
to be bathed by grace or made to be tolerant in unkempt rags of
the forgotten –
we are, yet, without respite, mere – and abundantly –
"lesser gods."

Elizabeth

early morning
February 25, 2015
– re-working an old, forgotten "part-song;"
great amusement – to rethink ideas which do not fly away
with the pirate of time –
but stay, to rearrange, even more the worthy –

Morning Images

I awakened, as a great, smoothly flowing water, into
another providing glory of mid–October,
at the coming to be in winter's breath,
the coldest hour, the four o'clock.
Immediately I perceived images, in their full colors and forms,
all about, passing, pleasing, queenly pomegranates largely round,
with satin smooth skin whose blemishes
appeared placed appointments,
waiting, like women of those already chosen;
Sunflowers, in graceful clusters, with
numerous varieties of companioning
centers, their bright being was equaled only by the remembered
fields of Goldenrod, grain to our soul, beauty
wheat in glory;
And the leaves -- soft fantasias drifting in memory, into the moment,
over years of patterns and colors like seasoned
dancers, not aged, but confidently graceful
in their long-time knowing.
My thoughts persisted, not to leave, not at table,
or among my books -- or attempts at other thoughts; these images
continued, retuning to me, and would not forgive until they were
captured by my pen.
We do not have because we have, in abundance, peace, and good;
but there is, of purpose, and design, beyond our grasp,
within the arrangement, a wager;
there is choice to have, and to not to have, and
not to have by reason of choice, alone.

In our lesser more, we envision, a paltry leften --
what then -- pour out that as the
pomegranate's scarlet blood, and bright or
cleansing in Sunflower lights,
to take away, in gracious good, this illusional joy --
freedom-heavy grief, flowing, into peace -- streams --
streams, deftly moving grace to blend, pouring
over onto, with the adroit movement of friendly winds.

Ah, Father, receive in Thy waiting breast,
always,
Thy Prodigal.

Elizabeth
October 18, 2015
six-fifteen am
Sunday morning, rising early --

A Day Past...

A day past night, full, with wishes of other days,
loneliness expressed as gratefulness
in acknowledgment,
and love finding familiar stones to step upon,
across to joyful touch –
the heart, in an oppressed stance, has forgotten
its fury, as shadows and dark chided its
continuing visitation, it acquiescing, finally, to softened
light, and cooler winds.
The restless heart requires an audience, whether quiet,
or conversational, and it is all of good that rapport brings
hope, to then a peace.
Existence of the outer round calls out physical
wants, and fatigued spirit, a season of reflecting, searching,
disrobing and decision – and then – only then –
is found a smaller place with winter's grey;
we can understand the heart's need to be spent with
summer radiance, filled and knowing,
looking toward the gold of harvest or
simply silent musings in the day's gift.
Man, thou "lesser god," to survey the encompassed circle,
to see and hope, to move with promise – ah –
satisfaction finds in knowing the fuller path.

– French parfumes,
the winter strawberry, a Naples' treasure;
gold from dearest family,
honor alongside saved resolve;
there be kindly women unto the day manifesting, yet most, at
nighttime,
and
Dew fall contentment reaches the far meadow –

Elizabeth
in deepest night, when medications could not hold or release –
June 30, 2014

much of the piece is unclear, with many improvisations,
in the morning, upon discovering the poorly written draft –

the line referring to "a Naples' strawberry"
is from Marlowe's "Faust" –

Episode Sentiments

Let bring to me early winds of morning,
virginal melodies of gentle strength,
that of the resolved feminine;
flame to me the promise, then, of sunrise,
and fling away, into
nothingness.
In these bitter vinegar and thorns, remember
to me moments of glory, of ease,
yet of scarlet passion that, if in my many times of
death, I live all over again.

Objectivity is truly not a construct if the
heart can contain mere token reminders while the
fuller soul breathes life into reason, until
both, at the first and last "I Am"
speaks a final peace.

Particulars are mere surmise, yet, in their own,
comforting.

-- pain in familiar, wanted step, but inside unableness --
weep, weep -- we forget more
than we remember --

Elizabeth
July 30, 2014
first thoughts on waking -- just before I became
ill (2014/ late summer), the episode
requiring, long, into the following spring --

-- better now, even nearly restored; transcription
in early morning hours, three twenty-five am--
May 4, 2015

Behind the Veil

Deep, Mediterranean purple, with threads
of finely spun gold;
and all about it falls a shadowing, to rippling,
as the light of stars, the flashing of a wealthy smile,
around a golden and leaping, demonic flame,
becoming a rubied glow:
A darkened veil hangs, before, and thoughts collect
hours in reason, wandering away to
struggle, waiting, before, behind,
and beyond, it a questioning of all time;
as we arrive to its presence, we wish to lift the veil,
but it requires, perhaps, more knowledge,
strength, and courage than – any, each – of us can be assured we have.
And if courage is in poor repair, possibly a vision, a voice,
or a prayer will begin its inventory.
We are of divine fashioning, but cannot, without
commitment, go beyond a hesitating avoidance of the responsibilities
necessary to accepting; it is this arrangement
which brings, into semantics, confusion;
prayer offered, personally, leaves, therefore, despair,
as the drape refuses to fall.
The thought leads back to the presence in mortal
flame, and mortal angst multiplies –
like a candle burning into a pool of its own self,
to eventually die;
we find a world behind with theoretical rose – responsibility
to only, again, stand a surmise.
On the outside we can see the inside; within, we can only know,
again, surmise.
We, then, become afraid for our acceptance, to beg grace, as when we
find understanding of our whole self.

Elizabeth
June 21, 2014
– on passing into sleep, thinking of the whole matter of death;
the script was almost impossible to understand, possibly
because of denial
and of coming knowing, but most, the press of
of fatigue, bringing sleep –

transcription completed early morning, June 22 –

Through All My Days

And I will love through all my days,
my humble grandiosity
quietly heralding, thoughtfully, each opened path:
to hold the moment, of a lifetime,
spent with he, of another;
to be on arm of the youth who is enamoured
of my matron beauty;
to wait the distance to he of the uncommitted,
for the distance is, now, only a step
away;
to hold as my soul's paramour, not in physical touch,
but in the sensuality of wisdom shared,
and thought, embraced.
Introductions always are about, good wit, and conversation,
splendid, very caresses of the perceived beautiful –
to find he who is frightened of the physical,
he who shares my love of beauty;
and he who is unschooled, but is aware of my
non-judgmental stances –
Ah, the heart is furnished so that it loves often, and deeply,
to be wounded just as so, but to be brought to
every height of feeling –
please, yes, yes, please –
"If I dance, I dance; if I die, I die."

Oh pitiable – I cannot advise my heart unto reason, for it is already
sentiment enthroned.
Let the Samaritan, then. cross over and, with grace, loose my fettered
heart, that I not longer suffer or allow woundings –
but yet, but yet – the absence of love – new love, innocent in its
firstness; love which conquers the impossible;
love which, in love, instructs;
love, with grace that we "lesser gods," can, repair and balm –
without these love – their absence
would wound unmercifully.

Elizabeth
June 24, 2014
in deepest night
– working, with effort, toward full assessment –

-- the life-long sentiment (philosophy of the exotic,
French dancer, the famous Isodora --
..."If I dance...."

The Dream As It Was Drement

Unsaid, unheard, yet not thought, let these
thunderous, these tortuous
realities sleep, again, their vengeful, leper
sleep, outside the walls of history's layered pain.
My heart is fatigued, moving in
mournful gray, with the loveliness of
paling spring, and the must processing
summer, lost to necessity, already, of a false ambiance of
coming radiance, lost to requirings that shout, that tear,
and burn the existenials to our descending home,
caught onto its golden chain, our home
which having always embraced, thoughtfully assessed,
if casting at times to the side -- and, if necessary,
concluded, in necessity's lack, to be
returned to olden patterns,
comfortably lived, other than among criticisms of
sameness, and lack of progressive bright.
-- or else may be we should altogether take
away this present identity, as it
impossibly is, seeking of noble cause,
individual justice, and license for all expression --
as it is combined, or in conjunction
with other modes of similar thought -- whatever the
rouse place aside which best accommodates.

A long path extends between idea and its
completed reality; how sad the product,
on arrival, and all of those spiritual others coming along the way.
Truth and the complete motivational impetus to its necessity is
a pitiable phenomenon we know of that we know, to do.
-- must, must -- the clarity of the mountain which
ascends, to point above the clouds: need we not take a sense of
its presence, and the fullness in the
accomplishing of its metaphorical lesson; come, Arthur's
words -- "Together, all, together this once... last...together...."
the dream as it was drement to become -- the fulfillment -- ought --
of we "lesser gods."

Elizabeth
mid-evening, thoughtful...
May 31, 2015
The work, Mort d 'Arthur is the source for the line of
Arthur's words to his knights (Christ to His disciples),
before the deterioration and death of the "Round Table"
dream. These words appear in the final meeting of the
"round Table" as "recorded" by Sir Thomas Mallory.

Insight

We need be as close to God as *we want,*
and *need,* <u>spontaneously,</u> and not for any alter cause
--not to force or press into a grotesque malformation
of redemption/salvation. Solitude and nature
will help the igniting movement
toward faith -- as will the soul giving up music,
and numerous other creative endeavors.
All that has been written may be instructive, but more, comforting,
balming or providing a pattern of behavior which can help
secure these, such admittedly, necessities
of living in peace.

Elizabeth
July 19, 2015
early evening

-- the writings of Saint Paul and many other
redeemed authors are helpful, necessary,
after a spontaneous commitment, but for many, a stimulus-response
salvation will not gather the peace of the heart -- only discharge the
need -- the I-Thou relationship cannot be
reduced to any pattern of words,
ritual, or liturgy, but a cognitively accepted sentiment between one
and his perceived spiritual presence.

Full Berry Hue

thinking, standing: in the wilderness,
whatever its fashioning;
or steps into truest gold, wealth immeasurable:
night and day –
raindrops cloudy and mournful, yet,
bejeweled countenance as Citrine touched by
morning light – to be a flower, fair and true,
is to lean on the breast of all,
for there is in thought, the complextion of
our climes.
Joyfully,
with impetus to move, the earth, and all therein,
is blessing to all of life.
The hands of children reach innocently –
as elder folk, though the elders' are marked by the wisdom of doing;
other hands bare gentle with the circumstance,
while some finesse their own ease.
But yet, and yet – in eveningtime, we survey
our day, and the passion of others is not so much
the histoire.

It has flown into each, our hearts, and whether
they become restless or content –
we know our cosem will color through
our eyes, only – andso –
we wait – for the day will follow the night,
and nothing, in wilderness or sunlight – is
greater than personal will,
it to enlarge, only when
all is embraced – to become, then,
full berry hue.

Elizabeth
midnight
June 2, 2014

Repertoire

At the close of day, pulling up the covers
of completion, and coming sleep,
our respite is often prefaced
by a small repertoire of reflections:
the grey, the intractable, the pressing clouded -- these
have been, in individual press, put aside, and we
smile at the sunshine's bright,
the final straight of the uneven path,
and the intermittent place at table
of the fuller feast.
As a mirror, our reflections show to us, before putting aside,
our fuller selves, for we take on an omniscient
stance as the day dies into tomorrow.
We feel our pain and know our fear;
we glory in the masterfulness of our own;
We weep sweet tears at the pace of time that crushes
the reflective mirror through which we observe.
But, though a surmise of our collected thoughts may arrive,
tomorrow is the wait we choose,
the dream we pursue, the enchanted wood which holds
our grails.
The covers safely sink into our encroaching
nothingness, and we travel
the path -- embrace the journey -- of we creatures, we "lesser gods,"
to enter the anti-chamber of day, a limberlost by reason
and sentiment, by will, and chemistry -- and
the crown of our being, hope.

Elizabeth
composed several days ago, transcribed tonight,
May 11, 2015

Yet, Wanting

A thousand, unseen bells ring in
the night's silence,
the thinker's words holding in my
thought;
realities crowd every perception,
leaving nothing but the darkness,
which, itself, is.
I reach and embrace all that I have,
and that is only all of me.
In these such climes rests purist self,
chosen, arranged, with effort, in place:
how ironic, how unhappy that it is as I want,
and is, yet, wanting.

Elizabeth
July 11, 2011
ten o'clock pm

content, if alone, but with a residual sigh, a yearning
I do not, at this juncture, fully understand –

Perhaps we do not know when we arrive at
truth – until sentiment, with press,
bests the lock.

Small Prayer, In Deepest Night

My portion, please, please, yes, please,
in the still of this night,
in the quieting of the wind;
in descending cold,
and constancy of dark –
let me know in these and in more, each
brief respite of the infirmities of
my body and spirit –
let, that the greater constancy, the
greatest respites, repose in Thy closeness,
and grace.

Restore to me, as Thou didst to him in recordings, old,
dressed in richest beauty
though my troubled faith does not impet of
dying family, and cattle, or losing wealth –
permit only the return, to me,
my strength and hope,
the joy of my salvation.

Elizabeth
in deepest night, in hard cold –
February 3, 2015

a small, spontaneous prayer, when rising to take
void of my aching stomach –
aching from the efforts of medication, that
symptoms, painful – in coldest night, a small
hour of winter season, 2014,
be forgiven –

Yet and Still

How to say, how to carry pain
on the embroidered wings of well-chosen words, those
whose arrangings create an ambiance of beauty and goodness
through rapport, serving ease. Yet and still -- dark and hurt
can become heavy wovens, lifting about through which the
weight of a spirit's breath is drowning in the nausea of
wounded soul -- in these vessels of sentiment, we live
and die, hours out wandering days -- and not so much
in lack of courage, but in its torture of carriage.
Sighs, and their accompanying, whispered
breath, are beautiful, in either their glory
or ashes --
but ah -- the true is that, more often than sun stars,
the golden pear's blossom of fragile ivory --
in autumn -- or the cardinal red of the master
bird, in uncommon circumstance -- more
often than these, we perish in the
tender grande of our glory.

Elizabeth
early afternoon
July 13, 2015

-- thoughts, and wandering mood, pressed by the
realities of held fancies, and the
clasp, yet grip, of the world -- inside,
and the outer must --

-- the world of "dinga, dinga," (things,
things) of Rilke, the now becoming
most renowned of German poets (yet Goethe);
Rilke was early twentieth century and
lived a very "unordinary" life --

Variations on Night-time

Night-time quiet is gracious, a lady of noble estate,
making all about -- gentle, soft, and without any governing
inequality.
Only shadows indicate life, and for the
close of chariot wheels spinning, voices, uncontrolled, and
violent movements that can sponsor in light --
such of night is good, such of night is
is, in its dew, good.
-- yet, so -- turning the leaf to its other side --
in reflection, and pensive mood, embracing
widened thought occurs in moments
such, destroying colored activity, as if it be present,
now, to this clay, the recognizable all, east of time true.
-- thought out this conscious graciousness --
dark, then -- and so, yet --
or, in all otherwise -- arrangements: "How many times will I die."
Dying is a lonely confrontation with time -- for it is individual, and
crosses, vestments, and pleading oblations -- these can only soften.
As appointments -- and appointments -- neither
do they always ease -- for we die
through variations of hurt and loss, yet
reflection, through time passing, through beauty fading --
just as surly as the ritual -- the hourly struggle, that of catching,
holding; expressing in respite; that lost to live, to leave all to those
who cannot know good -- the final glorious, the truest
equalizer -- the triumphant, closing breath.

Variations on Night-time

Night, oh night, when mischief can ride with
the highwayman and the kingly --
ease out life, quickly, into knowing -- blessed night --
be thy other visage, and fold close the heart that is kindled with
peace.

Elizabeth
in deepest night, with burking the ungood --

-- very ill, with heavy medication, thoughts,
a burdensome bramble --
December 1, 2014

Winter Image

In the full galaxy of steps, those issuing
out our nearly as many risings up and and lyings down --
if a pause is found in these,
within the quiet still of repassing greywine --
when some take refuge from the somber reminder:
in sleep, in small industries, or, when the
soul falls to its most desperate -- some become frenetic in
busyness, often appearing a glorious time of adventure --
and lovely -- becoming a creation of hidden, octavian sentiment.
From these circumstances, stories, narratives, small antedotes,
and yarns, (if stretched, at times, a length too far) --
these speak from former, worthy need,
as great as in their inception, or possibly more, in their present
recountings.
Characters and scenes, with particulars, as many as leaves
in summer, are redrawn -- slightly askew --
of their Eden colorings, but with
sentiment, sweetened by years, into centuries, yet eons -- nien -- so
what the matter --
Andso --
We live, more, as we relive then, and there is a
contentment within our togetherness.
These repeatings have been, always, and will, if hope continue remain
a construct of reality, to reoccur, for they are the flowing
soul of humanity, if in its unfated journey,

from ideas which all have truth, beside untruth;
and the cruel dissonance of the
in-between -- allowing pretense, embellishing, or excuse --
yet, abominable hypocrisy -- in the graciousness of giving shadows,
faith and good -- these all -- we, in our mortal half-guises --
half, left full -- the unbounded glory of life -- our hearts
to, in spectacular pieces, enjoy, beside sorrow, to be
forgotten --... "bitter, bitter..." --
as the winter grey, but sweet to the every taste --
left, it is our only own, and we love it, our certain true
of winter, our greyness -- in living movement,
in its still capture.

Elizabeth
musings, and, together, including their all, a full
bitter sweetness --
March 7, 2015
mid- afternoon
-- the words "... bitter, bitter..." are taken
from a small verse of Stephen Crane
an early (Civil War) author (American): novella, poetry --
untimely death, tubercular
The Red Badge of Courage

Thoughts...

How to bear knowing, and
feeling the knowing;
we look about, review our strengths,
and sadly understand that we will not
die, but will engage
all of it in full
cognizance, after some
fashion,
not yet to surmise even the medium
open to us.

Elizabeth
several days before
Christmas, 2015

Thoughts...

Anguish

Admonishing Shadow

Shadow, shadow, yet absent thought – into
the distance you find me, still: grey, with light of varietal
intensities, and, then, away with no
pattern of returning.
Wandering images – asleep, awake – leaving a heaviness,
or more, a compounded fatigue which bends and
bears open to let fall my precious coins from
my purse of spirit, into an unbearable
emptiness.
Beauty is, still, but it is separate to itself, not
touching, neither receiving, but must to be sought
out, and howso – the fatigue and its press,
inside shadow that does not review its grey beside
its lighted spaces, that a balance might be foraged.
The unmerciful, and pretender to peace, that awareness is,
yields a journey wide and rewarding when its host
is tolerant, malleable and accepting;
yet the issuing of the flow itself calls urgently, pleadingly, for the
hem of a garment whose reality is of many
textures, its presentation clear of a confusion of choice,
its origin and being with noble lineage and
credentials.
Shadow, shadow, dim into the away, and
let whatever is left to clasp and carry hope –
let, please, it to be kind.

Elizabeth
a very difficult day which has accomplished a kinder
conclusion, if still perplexing –
September 11, 2014
near midnight

"Bleeding Through"

I am I think -- I know, for I am "not" yet, by all objective
measures --
but what is being "am" -- for I do not feel -- I have
lived -- I think, and lost, I consider, but
I truly do not feel any but inertia, through senses or reason --
other than press of appearance: vanity is found
in and out of many pockets --
but more, not any but a nothing of emptiness, thankful for the
solitude of every moment -- the spontaneous
now of no requirement --
the richness of yesterday -- dead to movement,
the standing construct of tomorrow -- lifting mists and vapors.
Bells are still with me, but they do not
frighten or question -- they are only
a part of a new-found peace of either not caring at all, or caring
to the intensity of that unreal, not cognitively plausible.
Would the world I used to know be better, with this new wisdom, or
am I so lost to self, reflected out of the objective real,
that good and that not good are of no consequence.
I know I have felt, and deeply so, for I remember the circumstance,
but its reality has flown to the madness of Dido into
the hell of nonrecognition.
I have loved, I think, but distancing years have eaten up all of its
wealth, and I remain in a contentment I neither understand
nor wish, in most, whole truth, to continue.

-- thoughts in the night, with me now
almost always, in my repertoire
of sentiment, content in the sloth of accommodating unfulfilling --

Elizabeth
October 23, 2015
two-fifteen am

-- I am fully awake now, and frightened by this level's bleeding
through, and my companionable self, observing --

My wishes, today, are like my dreams that used
to be -- I just cannot know them
anymore -- other than attempts in the natural, and the
realization that there truly is yesterday,
and tomorrow, a fearful reality,
but not enough to care into doing -- there falls about an ambiance of
being "infused" into a reality that is becoming more foreign with
every thought: how many times will I die.

Full With Emptiness

I find myself inside a darkness, within
the catch of the bramble's knot, hearing the ditch that
often calls a familiar welcome.
The beauty of the day is now like an elegant
woman – a Beatrice, a Laura, or
perhaps, "Thee" of "...A Summer's Day..." –
all drifting away loveliness, an image of regal
drawings;
the day "compares" to "She," in the joy
of being – but a portion come, now relegated to the
great hall of memory – yet, truly, beside
generous content.
Andso, I find myself full with emptiness,
longings, yearnings, a grande pining,
a Shenandoah in holding, weeping for my lost
part.
The longing knows the distance to completeness,
the hours of struggle through reflection –
the freedom in oneness, concepted – but oh, the knowing,
the lost innocence in this
finding, a self of wholeness, in its becoming,
lost of need,
and that marvelous, of filling.

Elizabeth
January 29, 2014
one o'clock, am

a bit of insight, I think, in reviewing the day, in these hours
when the dark rose of midnight seals the day passed,
and opens the casement to a new promise,
the feast of another adventure – if the baton, alongside very
personal inadequacies, can be clasped –

– is the "enjoyment," just passed, "true," as that yet anticipated, or
an ideal finishing to some given particulars – perhaps best not
to place the diagnostic journal too close beside
coming spring – the "true" Romantic's nearly fatal strategy –

The various women from world literature are taken
from a course entitled, simply, "World Masterpieces,"
(first twelve lines of my verse) I taught at the
University of Mississippi College, Clinton, MS, three years
ago; It is as a lovely medley of beauty, grace, and virtue,
each serving different purposes for her author.

Dark Flowers

In the gentle solitude of midnight,
questing with gluing broken clowns,
my care separated out the task,
and beside my covering, yet, and still, active grief bent me.
Long-held images -- sentiments, bittersweet -- settings and
exchanges -- the lack of heart, throughout the day -- in
sound and touch, a glance, presence -- true -- these washed
over my defending movements into pain
unbearable.
Erie shrieks, of the dark macabre, mournful screams,
as those who know the knelling -- a kaleidoscope
of sounds -- red flames, dried crimson,
bight, flowing scarlet, touched by fire: dark
laughing flowers of Baudelaire:
these created an ambiance of more pain and I wanted it to
pull all feeling from me -- pull all from
me -- tearing flesh, bone, sinew,
that I triumph awareness, and die to knowing.
Like incisive wounds, I felt the blade, its full being, its absence,
yet blood drops from my breasts, burning,
pressing movements into my thighs --
the true exacting of my butcher lover --
-- and thrown like an enjoyed carcass, the ditch found to me smooth,
wet of dew fall, cleansing my wounds, my defilement. Such let me
die, for we do not ever live, not the full, for
hate and calloused laughter are
always at the Rose's stem -- a come, unfortunate norm of humanity.
Best to wither in fantasy's promenade, the recipe for
grace, with intense effort, before the abyss of
hell's fiery thought which can burn
through the full charade.

The deepest wound, the most sensitive to touch,
lies in the hurt of loss, that of the
quality of care that once gave voice to the breath of
life: understanding in silence, acknowledgment;
in exchanges, laughter in mutual ironies, and
tendernesses in gentle touch, passion dressing.
Caring is treacherous, softened with coverings, lovely, cleverly
critical -- finesses, trumps -- always, checkmate -- other
than the beautiful unknowings, the, infrequently, all of
ourselves into, not ever, in pain, to be forgotten.
We experience these, perhaps, within the dark flowers: the
pain, the diminishment, the clever slight of hand and eye
which lead to the level of knowing that the flame would
have been, if not better, close to absolvement.

Elizabeth
October 1-2, 2015
Thoughts from the day --in the cycle, up near
midnight with strength toward truth and
physical ableness -- perhaps three days -- with
each episode, more requiring;
I so fear my time in dependence in which I can see
what is to be, not to allow what might have been.

Baudelaiere was a very early, modern French
poet whose influence was extensive
among rising "malcontented" poets, including those in this country.

Full Decent

To descend is to move, to the below,
from that above to that beneath, in the between, momentarily or
extended, the curious real being nothing,
emptiness, to be incapable of being held.
Above is a reality – little girl in Easter blue,
further,
of perfection – rose, blanc, of she who is, in waiting, to he – perhaps,
walking into –
party to her greatest promise, her princess adventure;
or below, rich and porous, darkened wealth of cosmic growth
and beauty – bread and wine – seasonal preludes,
of life perpetual.
But the matter of descending is without those as
parameters, boundaries and such – only as
Satan and his "autumnal leaves,"
without, cast away;
if, yet, however, still is light: in thoughtful sentiment, cruel
strategies and receipt of sensation – but to be truly cognizant, against
no background, to allow the – with comparison/
contrast – reality to reveal:
descent is, then, in its being, the full of alone,
empty.
I cannot clasp, then, in these moments, neither hue, nor nutrients –
not, yet, if ever "yet;" – I am in descent –
though perception, some of true, some of half truth –
circumstance against will –
but is not perception, in a time, in a place, with attending
factors in the composition – is perception, not, with its particulars,
that most true, a knowing, meager, to we "lessers" in its aware –
I am, beside all qualifiers, in full decent –

Elizabeth

mid-morning, February 21, 2015
-- a difficult rising, approaching that tortuous, ought
than being softened by comfort through the
spontaneously, giving expressions of my pen; the small
reference to "Satan" and his "autumnal leaves"
is taken from J. Milton's epic of the fall of man, Paradise Lost --

Distances

Distance is an emptiness, a true void -- of a
"person, place, or thing."
It is precipitated by the breaking down of energies
given to a quality, an entity -- its departing.
We look at space, all that there is, floating between the
many of our realities, and distances bide the way.
Distance can be close, it can be further, and, more,
it can be to the away in a closeness,
somehow the warmth of the energies which bound
all together having lost the passion making one --
both individual, and alone, many, couplets, duets --
groups -- the trio. They do not know, anymore, the intimacy
once theirs, together -- lost, unaware, apathetic, unsung -- however
semantics can help.
A loosening of care, a lack of identity, a loss to
the oneness that only "distance" can
bring to be, the particulars abound, too
great to be ledgered, or recoded:
so great,
so removed,
so lacking in care:
"I will miss you the distance you go."
-- cold and still, unaware of any self, only the "self," but it, the fullest
individuation -- flown with the smoke of the fire
of love: the predominant, preeminent of all others, this
unique principal we once together were.

Elizabeth
November 16-17, 2015
-- a sentiment in the gathering ambiance
of the year's holiday season --

Distances may exist a lifetime, or very near
death; a week, a month, or until the
hearing of a familiar melody -- yet a reminded anniversary.
-- could be merely an abrupt break in friendly
rhythm -- but always, in reflection,
these remind the paramount position of that part of us that is
responsible for our being, continuing -- such with divine tempering
quite beyond mortal ("we lesser gods') understanding.

To Wander, Safe

Oh my self, my poor bramble,
hear my separated lamentations, those near the
flame, for I want to know the objective real,
the intuitive "yes" to the wish of
all of self.
The cumulative years of wandering in the limberlost
of the troubled real,
in the exquisite beauty of flowing dreams --
let come to the conscious which is my
constant plague:
a hiatus, a pause, a break -- then a balm to
the uncertainties of the objective,
the true of true.
Rest me gently with certainty born of genuine
want, of understanding the walk our steps
continue into.
Place a knowing that -- please -- is a deep, within the strength
of will: let repose untwine the knot that
constricts, always, ever was.

Elizabeth
October 13, 2015
just beyond midnight
-- troubled of much, most my perceptive stances, my
uncertain sureties which undermine my peace --

Of Gibran

My days do not, more -- most -- reach for the hour,
the sun's rising, the distance
between light and dark,
for clocks, and calendars, are seekers as well
as solitude, to my wholeness,
even pressing, if never interrupted, alone
of its voice -- alone.
The telephone, if just for sayings, is an archaic
instrument, and seasons without their
festivals, bear a sameness without their lovely markings: and to
complete the hierarchy,
animals, wherever in the arrangement, are neither
isolated or together in
every
moment.
We, are, all, compatible with silence, and sound, in some measure,
but the true tragedy is in the circumstance
in which one who knows his needs – in some holding insight –
but is not cognizant, in any completeness, of them.
His circle is continuous, and he, forever, with mourning,
is an island in unlabeled, unbearable truth -- most, to be forgotten --
in forgotten waters, its description to exist a dark,
drawn close, in unapproachable bramble.

Perhaps Gibran's quote speaks true:
"We make our own pain and sorrow long
before we experience them," (Gibran) – ("so much so that the
key is lost in the lock, impossible to turn,
helpless in opening,") – (Elizabeth)

Elizabeth
February 2, 2015
K. Gibran is the mid-Eastern poet who reached
much recognition during the
sixties (artistic work -- dreams -- and written
work -- (poetry) -- these of greatly
intriguing images and suggestions, in America
and about the entire of readers of poetry;
the Prophet is his most well known work, still much loved, today --

The Better Form

There is no moment too brief,
of which in its part, no glimmer of light issuing as faint --
that we do not hold in fancy or reality -- hope,
a measure of true good.
All is, lies within the quality of awareness,
in the abundance of this gracious gift.
If perception, colored by self and present, existential justice
-- the meadow, the pasture, the lane --
if these be -- all is possible, in faery
timelessness, by the transparent surge
of life, evidenced by joyful
constancy, yet, if the grande Natural pours out on us.
A coming, misinterpretation, however, can venture
forward -- bitterness from past hours --
these can inundate with a spirit of illness, and serve as a noxious
stimulus to be avoided.
Still, still it is he who is either silenced out that bequeathed
to the indigent we all house -- or quietly
looking to the better form --
a property, almost innate --
in him, questions grow and multiply at almost every juncture of these
statements, as the sage understanding the
cannoting of the seasons: the worded record
of our steps, our wisdom of the better form.
And the mustard seed suggests of peace,
but to the Augustinian king, the anguish of foreboding angst --
the entire matter of the always rising sun,
the benevolent and kind who

even crosses to the other side: these better form-- not
his want to choose -- this clouded circumstance
leaves the suggestion of
whatever unconscious knowing, through thoughtful struggle,
has offered a troubled image -- this increase, a partial
component finding in advance of the veiled
self, the better form to find
its beauty through pain.

Elizabeth
Thanksgiving Day, 2014

alone, still inside the larger portion of my most recent episode of
illness (both complexions), whose onset occurred in late summer --
thus, still a "bit confused" in my
growing "wisdom" --

-- I make reference to a paper that I delivered,
several years ago, at an arts festival
hosted by a fellow institution: "Giving
Pain: the Relationship Between
Bipolar Illness and Creativity" --

Prayer of Self

Contrary to most well spoken platitudes,
prayer is, in its most completeness,
one's communication with himself.
Our own domain, our only "pied de terre,"
is between the formidable fences of
awareness and denial,
with the constant walk, the steps which the continuous
movement of dissonance between;
the full aware has not always been,
as seldom now is the
future, it remaining, a mere surmise.
But the divine entry into all of us declares
the war of the trinity of knowing, unknowing, and dancing
our hours away, in our many frocks and sashes -- and
steps, fashionably adorned -- these between truth and untruth with
indecision, its constant vacillating, covered with clever
rationalizations: the polka, the waltz, the rondo --
andso -- for hours into days of years in the choosing of the
movement -- these rest toward or, against, the
chosen step.

Effort is noble, if honest and genuine, and these
qualities yield, if they do not harvest piety; but to
seek the true of self is to discover the All of All;
it is sweet, and it is sad, but its struggle, its reflective
constancy, within barbaric, but
beautiful fences lay us down in the peace
of the choice -- of no choice --
the riddle of the ages: acceptance, with a
gratuity of humility -- standing in
joy, within falling hours about, filled of a thousand white Gardenias,
now earthen brown, in color -- in fragrance -- a mere feigned
censorial reality, but with the abundant
knowing that we have
"walked these golden, earthly sands."

Elizabeth
August 3, 2015
just at bedtime -- thoughts --

August Epiphany

Tense, specific (static) or in flow, is in every moment,
and that of arriving, "being," is/will
always be "now":
and, if living in true wholeness --
a moment of acute realization,
moments of full awareness;
and times of pause, of still, do
occur, but are truly only reducing of the
movement, a re-arranging of the flow, not an emptiness,
a nothingness, not that fatally conclusive.
We need know this principle, else our breath, our voice of
life,
never be heard in its fullness -- felt -- experienced
as the cessation of a lover's longing.
This sense of urgency is not a complex, of covering,
of fugue, or displacement, but
an eager, joyful grasping:
Ah, to reach, Mr. Browning!

Elizabeth
August 20, 2015
breakfasting early, content, thoughtful
six-thirty am

the reference to "Mr. Browning," is to the
famed English Victorian poet, and
his very well known line from the verse, "Andrea del Sarto,":
"Ah, but a man's reach should exceed his gasp, or what's a heaven for."

Horizon Space

Our space is one within a larger space,
ours alone, to be added to, and,
soon, to be another space,
quite given over to time, a portion of all time,
with no beginning or concluding.
We become a myth, a fable, or perhaps, a small narrative.
but most, a reality, which slips
quietly – or with more or less soundings –
into a memory that can only be called
up, in most instances, for just the
"space of a hundred years."
Our portion of the whole is found with many
"importances," those some, a dream awake,
others, filled up and played out
visions;
but in a final analysis, we establish – grande, in some fashion,
or small, yet somewhere in medias – a narrative,
a script, a tale – to be our acknowledgment through
a century of Christmases.
Noble, yes, that out of struggle we began,
and increasingly noble that we conclude.
Perhaps we gave gifts;
perhaps we exacted recompense –
sad, sad – and in some
circumstances, sweet; That we did not take away
our masks, our contrived personae, becomes the greatest
sorrow, being our own ignorance of such, allowing
the false security of permitting others to
convince, press, or chide "we had a choice --
the choice that we made."

Elizabeth
Saturday afternoon, July 19, 2014
a recurring image, now several days – "as it came"

– the horizon can call, appearing a "very"
verity, but we also can perceive,
incorrectly, this behavior attributable to a variety of factors –
– the words and concepts associated with the term,
"horizon," in this verse, are taken from the early
modern dramatist's work of Eugene O'Neil': "The Far Horizon" –

The Magnanimous Gift

In these hours, my being alone is as a warm coverlet
draped about me, my entire person,
moving, a constant balm like oil pouring its softness, its
spreading fingers to tender touch.
For in my thought lies the mechanics of my
pain, and the great reservoir of yesterday, but also it
holds its forward appendage of hope, the bark
I cling to in these turbulent waters.
The scroll of remembrance rolls out before my
fatigued eyes, weary of pain, and
forced dependence; it does not chide, however,
for it is in my sentiment – the largest of my soul –
alive, again, with a glimpse of what
yet may be.

Divine comforter, my praise and thanksgiving
go out as a chorus of voices, sounding organ with horns,
for kin and friend abound, about, and many hands
offer in my way.
My petition begs strength, in clarity of thought,
in faith, to emerge free, on every turn, of the spectre
of doubt, that I see again autumn's smile, its refreshing
cool, and use my humble hands to fashion beauty
as monument to Thy ever care – all my days – the
circle filled, with grace,
Thy magnanimous gift.

Elizabeth
at noontime, in great pain, flesh and spirit
September 12, 2014

Morning Lover

Grandly, as light drew in around
the tall, stick-thin -- almost
legendary -- like spears of winter trees;
a mulled-grey -- gluevine spray all about,
a soft mist, the early morning of duel-hour
dressing --
these, my constant lover of changing robes,
moved tenderly
into my rooms, and I, in my covers, warm,
expectant, lay in content, and, at most, peace
of reason's pain, and all that is not.
And respite, somewhat, in the myriad symptoms of the
physical, my constant companion, of new late,
almost finding a continuing silence.
What joy of more, the beauty of yesterday, as today
becomes, in memory and lovely present.
Glory into glory in the mystical questions
of "When," "Where," "How." --
these sounded over, and over again.
What steps, in movement, increasing, each, its bright,
can be added to, or last, to sum, so great that be
as here/always: the now, then, afterwards -- into forever, eternity --
these, in each moment, present, aware --
this, be -- always; all other --
only a variety of surmise.

Elizabeth

on waking, watching the lovely coming in of first
Spring -- to me, a lover beyond worded description --
March 24, 2015
eight o'clock, am

Fullest Anecdote

In all fullness, I feel my glory,
the dark of night, the secrets of my heart;
fasting smallness, embracing the complete;
let contentment remind the joy in accomplishment of
the unknowing,
love with it small particles converging, to
become in the fore, to proclaim a victory
over all love –
though it be beyond measure or description.

First awareness, and the particular bent of
consciousness,
leading into an ambiance which can offer
everything or nothing –
the bridge or the abyss – the very gift of every day –
how not, then,. fullness, glory, a decided contentment,
if musings, aside.

The dark of night, the glow of sentiment –
portions of the divine, and their magnanimity –
incense, vapors, seances – these become
anecdotal to the prayers
of the knowing self.

Elizabeth
three forty-five am
September 18, 2014
a good day passed – if closeness to the inside of
pain and fear –

Tragic Flaw: Personae

When personae confuse, sentiment is undermined,
and reason is easily arrived, untrue.
In the wide somewhere of full existence,
we often mislabel, falsely qualify, incorrectly
attach meanings --
significance out logic, askew.
And -- the cosem we call our own, our small fiefdom, our
"pied de terre." -- our castle -- becomes gray and unhappy --
and there have been no walls, no gates or
bridges felled, as trees in wealthy forests,
no smoke from aftermath fires, no blood dried of its flow.
The confusion of personae rises out of
observation in bed with need;
we see what we wish and wish that we see. Reason clarifies
most often through priority, and the face, the voice, the
thoughts we come to wish deny into reason,
covering that once innocent, caught in the shadow of
only self -- the process of causality of this
circumstance, worn, tattered, thin,
now processed into new coverings which answer with apathy,
stimulation, and hurting exhaustion: a false, covering movement
which dies the once innocent into a brambled
half-truth, an existence "proper," perhaps -- fair and
true -- when the personae is in full view --
but empty when the self is examined, either intensely,
or in brief moments of interruptive insight:
unfulfillment when the feigned features are discovered, in
insistent solitude, that they have become individual flesh, true.

Elizabeth
December 6, 2015

-- an epiphany -- after having researched the
legend of the Christmas rose --

the theme is a distant memory of a piece read
in graduate school: becoming what we
find most time, being -- I do not quite remember --
something such as becoming what we overcome (Lear)/
or with every ounce of ourselves to become --
become only that
for which we have gasped --

How Many Times Will I Die

Times are, if most often not,
with moon shadowings into rising light,
an expectancy, so.
And they have about their varied entourages of
memories that enhance the glory of
awareness.
-- as gold, these hours image a similar
likeness, a treasure with its many flowers of joy,
and as with beauty, gifted toward good purpose,
but is with sometimes jaundiced perspectives;
unwanted judgmental stances, sloth in accepting fabled myth
and such, allowing to sleep the idiocy of a poor present, forever.
Yet is the whole, whether in reverie, falling distant, or
brushing the cheek, it is, however,
beautifully heavy with truth, in the embroidery of
yesterday --
is -- so -- saying, piercing in remembering, agony in
accepting.
pain, of thought or flesh, can be, also, kind, and in the very
weight of truth rests the invaluable strength of
necessity, prescribed, enhanced Samaritan support.
So then, the hours bide the moments of light, these
evolving, stretching toward, out this philosophic excellence,
this difficult dichotomy, a balance -- a sweetness, a
warmth stitched together of couraged weariness,
alongside a mourning, into a growing --
an unreasonable pining --
And to be -- a course of forward thought -- unfolded
the galaxy of paths, aware to the all of flesh:
we live in joy, within its many executions, royal and common,
into the constancy of death.

Elizabeth
mid-afternoon, May 10, 2015
-- a beautiful "Mother's Day," but... but
the sweet pain of the heaviness
of truth and beauty --

"... these golden, earthly sands...,"
two

Telling Evening Song

Songs, songs, come again, true to me,
dreams of once, fables, to be played out, into --
let the whisper of yesterday bring its lovely images that feed
my soul, as the seasons come, to depart into sighs
of time and being.
Sunlight, come, warm and bright, leaving cool shadows for reflection;
echo the color of night, its giving, free nothingness,
when the circle completes, with the
dreams that opened our awareness, to lie down
together in arms warm and twined:
presently -- content beside despair, these in royal blood reds;
sweetest grape wine, flowing, and gold of grain moving
in colorless wind, however, catching
the blue and pure of sky-- these against the ease of
flax and the fragrance of the rain cleaned, reaching-up earth,
Bamboo's green flame waving inside dark morning
light -- contrast binding our grief:
our gratefulness, our songs to return, the voice of breath --
the gift, in all its bounty (all of nature) and povertys:
the question, the search, wandering over into contemplation
and unknowing, aware -- coming wisdom and
truth -- the key to the lock of the
prophecy of eternity:
clothed in those of high born, and humbleness -- to
we who sweetly sing our faith and doubt,
infinite, unbounded truth, clothed in humility, with glory --
salvation's grace.

Elizabeth, Sunday, July 5, 2015
near midnight
-- the accepted, perhaps contrived holiday, weekend -- any day --
I and me, and all of me; all of me -- all that I have,
and have to be--

The Contemplation

Much of our days provides moments for contemplation,
whether in friendly woodlands, the
springtime greenscape, below its lament of the
Southern mourning dove;
in demanding traffic, which lulls;
or in a lethargic grocer line – our consciousness
is tireless, finding adventure holding paradox, juxtaposition –
irony – a nearly touch with representative humanity.
Eternity flows in and out the reality of now,
and we ought, must to be humbled
at the wideness, yet the pressing of the matter of being.
It may be that we have forgotten too readily,
and recognize too little, but in the face of need, in
the matter of wounding, in moments of joy and praise –
if these can come to us, to our recognition
at some level, so that a memory bears, a somatic
response ensues, a comment, under breath – quite
unknown to the self – is expressed – we are, indeed,
on the threshold of a fullness, a peace,
and understanding; spirit is greater, in these climes,
when flesh and that of a man which lives, breathes
but the blessing.

Elizabeth
– written at twilight on Saturday, before Easter, April 20, 2014;
the peace of my rooms, looking out, and backwards into a beautiful
day, has evoked these comments –

The foremost antidote to despair is looking "straight" into
the present moment of being.

In this, my "cosmic slice," I accept what is, that I can know.
six thirty-five pm, April 19, 2014

Jaundiced Passings

The seasons can be placed together, for they are,
in these lovely hours, found in each other's
company, to pass away, quickly,
their separate visages.
Summer's contained radiance, and autumn's anticipated
completing bear, metaphorically, beautiful in
the blood scarlet bright of the farewelling Geranium,
above the feminine softness of a king's feathered gold, wandering
Chrysanthemum.

In what fashion may I tender my expressions so that these
beauty not be marked with shadows of grief;
how do I feign purist smiles and joyful touch when it is the hard of
truth which brings these patterned hues into grief's awareness –
my tears of knowing loss, discordant sentiments
in wretched houses, and, bending under full cognizance
in visiting reflection – of that no more that was, but more, the
complete lack of possible redemption in the
final, sounding silence –
These wounds fall with my glances, to consenting blossoms,
in my clasping hands – these beauty cannot but receive the
sayings of my heart.

The morning's jeweled dew fall is joined to the seventh heaven
as the afternoon's pasteled rainbow has gathered
into the wide of sky;
and the pain will enter a consciousness which
cannot, though without stain, yet be put aside.

Elizabeth
October 9, 2013
ten-thirty pm

a day of unhappy circumstances, those present, and in thought –

Come Innocence, Full

Somewhat a lighted, soft bubble,
I move through my rooms, now my cosmos,
just from the potter's wheel,
peripherally bounded by the innocent beauty
of early summer: green, lighted;
colorful smiles of fragrant rounds and stars;
winds, gentle, and the lovely sound of dressed
solitude.
Inside this new womb of growth, the press of its
coming -- winter blasts -- the dormant seed,
the pouring wine of grey -- is somehow laid aside,
and ideas within the all comfort
of this newly arranged feast enjoins me to the former
self I perceive I, of certain knowing, was.
My purpose is to feel and know, in awareness, content,
to arrive to a naivete, productive -- knowing which will
allow the peace of worlds that only flowers are.

Elizabeth
-- in deepest night, following a difficult day
April 29, 2015

within soundings of the air, "Pippa Passes":
"God's in His heaven, all's right with the
world." -- Robert Browning --
-- a good day to follow --

Waiting Ease

For each small peace that comes to me,
conflict either out disquieting struggle, or from the hands
of another, I offer great thanks.
Being dark, yet, and the cold of mid-October pressing in,
I am warm and safe in my pleasant rooms; pain is
not in great presence, yet, and
medication has found its hour.
Turning the lamp, gifts of color, a very kaleidoscope
came, bathing me, with its exclamations;
and I have awareness and capacity to
receive these. Perhaps even more gracious is memory of their
arrivals – hours, days, and special moments filled
with the joy of reproducing beauty – from the natural, from
thought, and image extravaganzas: stars, bells,
and flowers – I smile to catch these
words – "toys" that rose from out my musings
of the, always, triumph of life.
We are not strong other than in keeping
the long journey of acceptance of the ambivalent
stone: pain and ease. We are most weak in
the denial of such, it causing thrashing
about – inside our hearts, touching others, and
withholding knowledge so that even larger
movements of the ungood flourish.

– out moving, grey mists, and shadows of thought levels
unknown, but influencing conscious activity, at some later
time –
early waking, small light, still silence so that thoughts can wander;
-- perhaps a dream from deep sleep within can be found taking form:
in spiritual bartering, the feast of today is adequate
exchange for, yet, another awareness of the uncertainty
of eternity --

Elizabeth
waking at four o'clock, am, mood, good –
October 20, 2014

the reference to the "ambivalent stone" is
from "The Myth of Sisyphus" –

Tragic Beauty

Waking just after midnight, in deep thought,
and, always, my spirit ought, most, but pulled
down -- I was found, still, able to be
careful of the hour, the day, and
future waitings.
But in the assessment of only a breath,
I knew the trough in which I lay.
I could see two, nebulous rounds, side to side,
orange and burnished gold; they were afloat, but, yet,
eventually always together: downy soft, new feathers or, if often
a possible sigh for the self, only its own to know.
These images were similar, and also dissimilar
to all others; and I knew that, also, in their unique
beauty, they were, among, as all others.
I saw, as I always have seen,
the eventual triumph of life. But with struggle, grief,
reaching – to clasp – and brambled thought – into a
metamorphosing we cannot know,
this be -- with Cana's catching touches of light.
I was reminded of the lovely swamp moth,
and its passion to veer close to the flame.

With its particular qualities, everything is caught between
other properties – giving, and, most, resistive; we clasp the
giving, and pursue the rest of the way, grateful for even small
reprieves – the tragedy of the beautiful in life.

Elizabeth
December17, 2014
thoughts, while pushing sleep away –

The Quatrain

I hear through echoes;
I see within halos;
I feel inside memory –
my being is afraid of the true, the real.

Completely unencumbered, escaping description –
location, understanding, evaluation –
I know inside these appointments to my
nature, the freedom of a self –
it is sweet, and it is sad, as love out of
definition in prescription.
Color, sound, and movement through light and
thought engender fatigue, however yielding
an awareness that is like meeting
my self, and finding a good companion.
We are, over time, as we always are, yet a self in
the Caterpillar's pocket.
Almost mystic longings, concrete realities – these which press –
come, come sweet peace – found, left over
a day, reason in memory, inside which
nothing is added to, or taken away, only reviewed,
and accepted, sighs falling,
catching back with eager hands, all that was.

Silver and distant blue,
ivory bearing marks, touched of time –
who I am is only a surmise,
a construction of forces,
these upon other forces, one of which is will.

Elizabeth

– beautiful climes, today, if cool – I am not
sure if another Spring is come;
freely associating inside coming sleep –
March 20, 2014, the first day of Spring, if by the calendar;
one o'clock am, March 21, if by the clock –

Sacred Loss

I am aware, and in clouded fashion,
concerned with a new consciousness.
I have come to need, more than not, little other
than that, presently, in my hand;
my goals live within the day, and my glance is more
than, sometimes, to the hindward, always
before towardward, if insisting yesterday close beside.
My many passions hold, still, within me, yet their presence
quietens, mercurially, and a different cause
now speaks with a repeated credo.

Am I fatigued, or simply more wise – or perhaps,
at last, stoically resigned.
Flowers continue to reach into my heart as
does the new morning's freshness, and if my
solitude did not, only occasionaly, press – the absence of
others' laughter could grieve me.
But in my steps, in my thought, I find a knowing –
of my dreams, my beautiful and worthy dreams – I grieve
the loss of their fire,
their sweetness, the purposed steps a romance of
dreams can weave.
It may be that the greatest loss I can know
is this ambiance, holding: those,
almost sacred, now somewhere, out of me, and I do not
feel the need to reach, more –
if could be, could be – a small afterglow –
a dream, sacred, in itself.

Elizabeth
May 25, 2014
early afternoon, alone – and, almost, not lonely

Behind the Veil

Deep, Mediterranean purple, with threads
of finely spun gold;
and all about it falls a shadowing, to rippling,
as the light of stars, the flashing of a wealthy smile,
around a golden and leaping, demonic flame,
becoming a rubied glow:
A darkened veil hangs, before, and thoughts collect
hours in reason, wandering away to
struggle, waiting, before, behind,
and beyond, it a questioning of all time;
as we arrive to its presence, we wish to lift the veil,
but it requires, perhaps, more knowledge,
strength, and courage than – any, each – of us can be assured we have.
And if courage is in poor repair, possibly a vision, a voice,
or a prayer will begin its inventory.
We are of divine fashioning, but cannot, without
commitment, go beyond a hesitating avoidance of the responsibilities
necessary to accepting; it is this arrangement
which brings, into semantics, confusion;
prayer offered, personally, leaves, therefore, despair,
as the drape refuses to fall.
The thought leads back to the presence in mortal
flame, and mortal angst multiplies –
like a candle burning into a pool of its own self,
to eventually die;
we find a world behind with theoretical rose – responsibility
to only, again, stand a surmise.
On the outside we can see the inside; within, we can only know,
again, surmise.
We, then, become afraid for our acceptance, to beg grace, as when we
find understanding of our whole self.

Elizabeth
June 21, 2014
– on passing into sleep, thinking of the whole matter of death;
the script was almost impossible to understand, possibly
because of denial
and of coming knowing, but most, the press of
of fatigue, bringing sleep –

transcription completed early morning, June 22 –

Waiting Glory

A full flowing of beauty came at the
earliest entrance of light;
like a queen descending, to be seated
in her waiting glory,
the day of resurrection began.
Hours processed, moments knew small
splendors, and at beautiful
parameters, the magnificence of spring
was come.
Time, gracious, exacted all that was,
and as the afternoon grew,
reflection, courting the gradually concluding
sunlight, began the feast to come again.
And finishing twilight blessed the
venture,
the day whose bright is commanded by
Dante's stars, God's presence, His warming
love shown to grace us all.

Elizabeth
closing Easter Day, 2014

– the verse covering the anguish drawing a wish
that should have been –

the reference to Dante is from *The Divine Comedy, part, the Inferno* –
"stars" appear throughout his work, indicating the
the warmth in God's love – a lovely metaphor –

a true knowing of the passing of time, prompting a verse –

Elizabeth's Findings

"Come Back," -- fragment

Come back to me,
moments,
hours, present days
of expectancy, promise --
joy imagined:
these sustaining avenues
of blessed hope,
yesterday's feeding nourishment,
today's tomorrow's dreams --

Elizabeth

an older fragment, written in 2010, found in these
present days, and here transcribed from the handwritten
note --
July 14, 2015
eight o'clock am

Dark Questions

The questions we ask, ponder, to then often cast
away, in contempt, grief, or
impotent new beginnings --
those are not ever to be answered as responses to the
questions we verbalize.
We objectify our open sores so that the balm
of inconclusion is all that can be the answer,
allowing still another tease of finding truth when we
always know not to unveil the cancor of
fatalism --
as the world, these present calendars can present.
There are innumerable steps between the finite
and the infinite, only one all
complete without any relative questions,
and we foolishly search out the one, with random wishings, to
appear astounded at the ineptness of
completion,
game playing becoming the natural, the "normal" act of
living -- to not do so -- how not to do so --

Circles and saucers, seasons and the bronze king
with his companion, the silver lady,
-- in all correctness, salute! -- of itself, into itself,
but most, so, in different stances of flesh, that upon any one
example of attention given.
And so then, why does my spirit grieve, and mourn,
into pining, besting wait, the, having only
light to gift laughter, the lark in the meadow --
the laurel of graceful leaf, the faint of truest love.

All is well, then -- no -- we abhor the burking of
sameness, and dream dreams of young men -- yet --
while there is the hour whose purpose is to give our joy,
in flowers of even darker laughter - a skewed existence -- the
"snows of yesteryear": those values yield a
wish to bring together in "one more content."
The paradox of self, inside a world yet unaware
of multiple inconsistencies, irregularities, and
hard untruths-- how, before we can close -- is the tranquil
peace for which we work, we wander, and we dream --
to finally, humbly pray:
"Lord, have mercy; Lord, have mercy; Lord have mercy."

Elizabeth

a prayer at bedtime after many episodes of
cyclings -- where is the shade under the trees, across the river,
where we may lie down....
Ernest Hemingway, *Across the River and*
Under the Trees; American, twentieth
century novelist, referencing the dying words of the beloved
Southern general of the Confederacy, "Stonewall Jackson" --

-- second week of June, 2015,
in deepest night, concluding --

For the Moment

It sounded out, like the knelling
of a death, for I know it is in place,
and will be.
My individuation, my penchant for freedom,
has turned back on me, and
in, now, complete bondage, I stand, alone.
I had thought, in recent hours, the muse
had left me, that I could no
longer "say,"
but in these deep, night hours, conversely,
the early, new day,
my shield, my defense slept in my sudden
waking, and all at once, I knew pain, the elixir
to my songs, for the reality of my
will's marriage to circumstance, provided; in a deft
maneuver, circumstance secured its prize, and I stood, of will, only,
and with circumstance, alone, into full awareness:
then, again, the dammed again – the refrain,
"no voice, no touch, nor, yet,
any thought for me."
"The mind always protects itself" – a familiar
construct – still, in this circumstance,
cognition's fare was
without honor, and less of will;
in nauseous despair – the battle was, for the
moment, lost.

Elizabeth

four o'clock am
May 25, 2014
– inside the Memorial Day weekend celebration,
the first full day of summer –

-- holidays -- always "alone days" -- so --

Shield and Bulwark

I sat alone in old darkness,
we together in the
shadow of the moon.
The chorusing silence, its smoothness
and tolerance, moved the hour into new
morning.
How do we know the night or day, yet before or later –
these are colorings of the aware.
The portioned self reveals the warmth and passion
possible, but circumstance tempers
this revealing, in greater moments;
we look, then, and find that which light
does not illumine, to keep
within ourselves the musings of our hearts:
the light and dark, the night giving
over to breaking day.

Elizabeth
May 20, 1014

thoughts while preparing for sleep, with responsibilities
in the morrow; I stand in awe of our thought
potential, the mind always protector and
bulwark of strength to itself –

Within the Urn's Call

What of will, when in full knowing:
a pale complextion in the loss of hope,
the circumstance of most dark –
And what of time passed, the verdict of yesterday,
of that lost which never was;
ah, to be burned with an energizing fire,
a brilliant flame, consuming, leaping; or to
be ravished of purist desire –
yet to succumb and lie spent, with spirit
in weeds of all blackened hues –
A fancy, an ebonied romance whose hearts glow,
a satin's black, in unable light;
shadowed words, a tale of deepest night,
when cognizance cannot hold the complete of
consciousness;
let come, then, the loss of all, letting go the pain –
the full pleasure left.

Elizabeth
April 16, 2014
eleven o'clock pm
after a difficult day of assessing, recognition, and
unhappy acceptance –

I Will Try To Think It ...

I will try to think it, the last, the final moment –
the judgment – or the full nothingness,
if there is a nothingness;
in place, how far, or how, conceptually, the
parameters –
eternity: more than a word, the clever
game of semantics – when there is no measure,
how can the unmeasured be.
We stand and are cognizant, but without cognition,
where are we except away from what
is reasonably in place.
Perhaps I cannot think it, the last and final moment,
only to experience it, not to be retold,
collectively, they all, an arrangement we
cannot conceive, but accept: myth, fable
or a void in thought – the defense of us "lesser gods."
But then, if void – where, or what is the "not"
that makes the void – without memory,
There is no yearning, no construction of what
was, or might be – the river into the sea, all one part
in divisions, not separates which wish to re-connect –
individuation is a curse,
making a supposed possibility of choice –
there is only the maneuver of acceptance which
leaves the all together, and any movement is the aware
ranging of what always was.

We cannot understand; there is no approachable Eden, no
salutation or amen. Praise is recognition of
glory perceived, but remains incomprehensible –
acceptance, without words, of the feast, and the
moment when the table is no longer accessible.

Depression, sadness, regret – these exist
because we are taught of the reality,
choice. If there be any choice, it lies inside
will, a quality as indescribable as nothingness, and, more,
at the hands of circumstance.
Deep into myself I find questions which have no answers, for there
is nothing other than will and circumstance, and they spar
inside the magnanimity of wherever it is that control is seated.
And "hope is the forward appendage of thought."

Honor, courage, with faith and hope – perhaps these can help,
but best to wear two shirts to keep the cold from
giving the appearance of fear.

That we spend time looking or thinking far into ourselves may
be a braggart's suggestion that there is a self, far into,
and a simple trust that the self, whatever its composition, is secure –
that it is – may be a worthy conclusion without all of the
answers.

I am alone, a circumstance to which I have significantly
contributed; I feel almost powerless to
re-connect or, yet, wish to do so –
I do not, then, think, further;
there is a portion of ease in sloth –

Elizabeth

an incomplete piece of free association, during the week
of Easter, 2014

Admonishing Shadow

Shadow, shadow, yet absent thought – into
the distance you find me, still: grey, with light of varietal
intensities, and, then, away with no
pattern of returning.
Wandering images – asleep, awake – leaving a heaviness,
or more, a compounded fatigue which bends and
bears open to let fall my precious coins from
my purse of spirit, into an unbearable
emptiness.
Beauty is, still, but it is separate to itself, not
touching, neither receiving, but must to be sought
out, and howso – the fatigue and its press,
inside shadow that does not review its grey beside
its lighted spaces, that a balance might be foraged.
The unmerciful, and pretender to peace, that awareness is,
yields a journey wide and rewarding when its host
is tolerant, malleable and accepting;
yet the issuing of the flow itself calls urgently, pleadingly, for the
hem of a garment whose reality is of many
textures, its presentation clear of a confusion of choice,
its origin and being with noble lineage and
credentials.
Shadow, shadow, dim into the away, and
let whatever is left to clasp and carry hope –
let, please, it to be kind.

Elizabeth
a very difficult day which has accomplished a kinder
conclusion, if still perplexing –
September 11, 2014
near midnight

In Our Knowings

--summer days, those long, and
quietly still,
the sunlight in absolute glory --
and then, in comparable qualities,
the tranquility of the coming
gloaming:
if we forget, and can pause, and
our thought holds,
we come to weep, into exhaustion,
bent,
in less, and more;
no written word can
say
the sentiment:
how old, how old we become, yet, are --
in our knowings.

Elizabeth
Sunday afternoon, five o'clock pm
July 19, 2015

-- having had a long phone conversation -- a very pleasant one --
with David, always to be my "little brother," of great
love,
still --

Tragic Flaw: Personae

When personae confuse, sentiment is undermined,
and reason is easily arrived, untrue.
In the wide somewhere of full existence,
we often mislabel, falsely qualify, incorrectly
attach meanings --
significance out logic, askew.
And -- the cosem we call our own, our small fiefdom, our
"pied de terre." -- our castle -- becomes gray and unhappy --
and there have been no walls, no gates or
bridges felled, as trees in wealthy forests,
no smoke from aftermath fires, no blood dried of its flow.
The confusion of personae rises out of
observation in bed with need;
we see what we wish and wish that we see. Reason clarifies
most often through priority, and the face, the voice, the
thoughts we come to wish deny into reason,
covering that once innocent, caught in the shadow of
only self -- the process of causality of this
circumstance, worn, tattered, thin,
now processed into new coverings which answer with apathy,
stimulation, and hurting exhaustion: a false, covering movement
which dies the once innocent into a brambled
half-truth, an existence "proper," perhaps -- fair and
true -- when the personae is in full view --
but empty when the self is examined, either intensely,
or when in brief moments of interruptive insight:
fulfillment ensues when the feigned features are discovered, in
insistent solitude, that they have become
personally, irredeemably flesh, true.

Elizabeth
December 6, 2015

-- an epiphany -- after having researched the
legend of the Christmas rose --

the theme is a distant memory of a piece read in
graduate school: becoming, what we
find, most time, being -- I do not quite remember --
something such as becoming, in true flesh, an overwhelming
identification (what we, perhaps, have overcome (Lear)/
or, with every ounce of ourselves to become --
to become, only, that
for which we have grasped -- with no
sentiment left left for redemption --

Acceptance

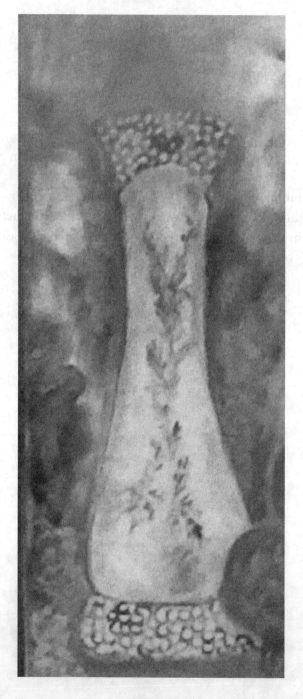

Morning Prayer

In patient review, within late hours
of early morning,
I know, again, the gifts held
from the spent day, resting in kept silence.
And I continue a refrain, close to a
simple, and complex, hymn:
"How do I love Thee, for it is always,
to love Thee."
All praise I find in my heart, with petitions,
small, for Thou art a "good God and lovest
mankind."
Early dew reaches up, and trees, in their all
nobility, gaze, with a quieted passion, upward;
the sun's rays spread outward, and
down to the earth, to be reflected back to the
heavens in the smile of the rose.
Night embraces all, the gentlest of coverings,
falling, to then fold itself up - to bear open,
in time, Thy fullest face in new morning.
These, all, humble gestures of
greatest care, I gather to myself, and
with them, join-

to love Thee.
Elizabeth
in deepest night
May 21, 2013
3:40 am
Of spirit comes my love, my praise,
quite beside the harsh realities at every turn;
there is no answer, for there is no question –
only to clasp the moment,
which being, is all of good,
and, therefore, beautiful.

The quote beginning "for Thou art..." is from
a prayer in the Russian Orthodox Church offered
by Father Paul Yerger, Clinton, MS.

Scripted Repeat

In the deep of my knowing own,
I am sad to myself tonight; I have said too darkly, and
spoken of tears, indication of their, if gathered,
filling the most grand urn of all lands'
fabled genii.
But the heart is loved, truly, with most fervor, of its own host, and
more, in most of the real world's singulars, they to themselves, so
that another, alone, cannot come in, to gather
away the tears of first pain or
those of valediction -- not until -- not unless --
all tears fall from similar fonts, the rose out perception
that is both, closely, finely tuned to hope
and requiring circumstance.
Oh, in my selfish, my pressed individuation, renewing
innocent need -- I have fancied that a Rose
of worthy lineage will offer to catch one of my tears
into a togetherness of fragranced
Almond and Cherry.
Ah, foolish, ever, ever innocent: still holding in
the matron heart --

Elizabeth
in deepest night
March 23, 2015

-- spring is beginning its cover of the lost radiance of a faintly
remembered summer, to a new radiance of its
small eternity -- yet to gold flowing over
to be supplanted, in spirit touch, always concluding with the
scripted repeat --

the rose metaphor is a statement of a physician
(plastic surgeon) with whom
I consulted, some few years ago, in Jackson, MS.
I have remembered this phrase, and its generalized wisdom (Oriental)

"Every operation is not a rose."

Coming In --

The dew fall, the raindrop, the autumn
butterfly in paling bronze, with ebony veins -- ah --
then gathers fresh moist as of breath,
together -- with early eventide -- exquisite transparancing,
if ephemeral, clinging in tenuous, fragile strength,
to hold until death of beauty and courage.

Thoughtful microcosms of we, our day,
its importances, to be arranged:
to build temples, walls, and
cities, and in doing so, also, to sail large vessels,
play the falcon, pit the beast; study, in cold cells, to then pray --
to record, and die -- but not until the power of sentiment has
embellished the violin found in ideas and
thought -- love, passion of many colors,
honor, and loyalty; dissonance into forgiveness, alongside
the lightly touching, idyllic bronze in flight,
bringing a season -- it coming in --
be kind in its revelations of the marvelous now, moving into the
sweetness of yesterday, left the
hopes of tomorrow -- the grail, perhaps,
surly, the feast of the quest.

Elizabeth
November 4, 2015
thoughtful, just before sleep, the review --

-- early morning -- casual, but light fatigue,
allowing jocund moments, of
smiles it bides --

In Times

In times when sentiment falls about like the golden
flax that faeries weave,
my dissonance is oppressive, beyond the
voice of life, for many knowings
cover our consciousness -- could be
poor metal with silver, with all of their different
accompaniments, finding reconciliation by the deep,
wide reaching pulsations of kindred hearts.
Perhaps I should have stayed, or if to
leave, to have made a change grande, deep, a traversment
not ever thought, again, to be healed.
And in going, I should not have looked back --
for in such is an Achilles' wound. It may be that had I
stayed, flowers in all their simple, woodland
glory should have been enough, not
requiring climes of different lineage, against the walls
of the cultivated passing of time.
-- but the Poppies -- the worded descriptions,
dressing truths, not truly
foreign to me, but sustenance and evidence to my soul.
Beside my going, drift the faces of my little
"brownskins," in play and finding -- they into a level
more comfortable -- less hurt -- but a delicacy of
homesickness that is made a tolerable one to me --
in the breath and width of understanding -- knowing, feeling --
yet, together, the
many faces, the wealth of the multiple paths to God.
Evaluations are difficult, for reason is like the
stone, and sentiment, the early petal; to marry them into
a good peace is an act of hurting courage, release,
and reconciliation.

Elizabeth
Thanksgiving Eve, 2015

-- after long, requiring sleep of sadness, but the drape of
the past is slipping into a well-earned content,
if one without and with; going home is reaching the
comfortable forward --

Mortal Secret

When summer winds, in morning hours,
blow shyful, yet with cool into warm,
and coming twilight brings shadows, early,
anticipation rides on refreshing movement
and we sense the passing of a season, the advent
of another.
An energy is somehow created, as if in its firstness – the sleep
of Morpheus being thoughtfully skillful –
but in my heart of secrets, there is, in sum,
a composed mourning, a small grief, a reflective sorrow;
for the earth is old, with now time, and before time;
many – more than can be numbered – have walked its
various surfaces – these all unknown to us, most only
through thoughtful awareness. And we embrace,
almost with an intense haste, the
dying radiance of summer – melon colors, peacock
elegance, nights of very sensual touch – but,
with a longing for gold, sienna, and umbers, we reach
for harvest which softens the reality of inevitable
winter.
Conclusions, inside careful thought, compliment, and
appoint coming beginnings for they both
speak of the one, closeted adversary, the gravest
wager, mortality: we the only creatures, alone,
who know.
We clothe this truth with myth and fable, with "mental
gymnastics," with assuming the behavior of the hound of heaven –
to run toward whatever would be a hiding place;
more often, perhaps, fatigued with the wrestling,
we simply lay it aside to a more convenient time –
carrying, allthewhile, the burden, certain.

The final turn is clever, if ironical; it is simple, and
yet, the more difficult: and herein lies my secret — there is
redemption in acceptance but also the giving over of a portion
of our mortality, surly the mirror which echoes back
our all of beauty, and grief.
Acceptance does cushion defeat, and personifies truth
to all explorers. It is just that it requires the
complete of one in the moment, alone, for that
is all we can have, all we can experience.
It is inside the boundary of now, and is already departing
its present, at awareness.
If, then, as "lesser gods" we give all fealty
to present awareness, that such as
seasons, days, years — eons would be ours as we walk, to
step through to a moment, of eternity, out
the heart of a moment in time.

All that was, is nevermore, for we have stepped
past time and space, all of the reality that was once,
now into a moment that is eternity.
The moment of mortal hopes and dreams, with their
inward treasures, will be in forms passed;
we will have slipped into the
moment, eternal, a separation we can express, but not
truly know.
The angst accompanying this knowing reaches deep into
my secret, and from the only perspective
allowed, makes mine even into more.

Elizabeth
thoughtful, about much
September 20, 2014
near eight-thirty pm

Gravest Struggle

Perhaps the most significant battles, those most
grande, if unrecorded,
are fought within the small, uncharted hours
of the night.
The legions included are not of those with glint of
steel, whose passion is chorused
by drums – these surrounding – but in the single, the only self,
naked before its person.
There is a total fierceness, dissonance and clarity,
together; a savagery that does not
flow blood, but a bending, into bowing –
to circumstance, one's lack of prowess, or the lack of
enough strength of will in it.
But a cognitioning, an accepting bearing, to
the full face of truth, the reality of others, and that of
one's own is called out.
To see one's self objectively, or in some manner,
disguised, if inconsolably, unreal –
is an encounter that must its struggle in solitude,
and all the strength of the latter,
with the full regalia of the properties of the self,
to struggle into victory or loss.
The night is long, and with a taking silence, if washed of
deepest dark; and the inclusive hours, in their length, are
requiring –
yet, is possible – if strength of self is present –
to arrive into an open awareness.
There is no greater battleground, no maneuver toward victory,
however able, but that of seeking truth – and therein
lies the pain, the blood of open flesh,
the cry for mercy, it to become, in selected
arrangings, a triumphal expression
of victory.

Elizabeth
January 3, 2014
in deepest night

a theme written into verse, simply, in the late 1960's, at Ms. Walden's;
the circumstance in which I found myself
dressed the early verse: illness,
heavy medication – alone –

Redrawn

But the gilded, old clothing of the scourge,
will find dark lustre in the
sooner than later, fundamentally
besting peacock gold and harvest multi-hued shadings --
and the dance come round again,
with, and into, without the Rose, the
sunbeam, the strawberry.
What then, but to imbibe once, perhaps another,
and take on the grace of age
that finds acceptance in the lovely-colored,
many-textured true -- but also
somewhat false -- enough, still, that we can, yet,
hold to the glory
of the feast.

Elizabeth

concluding "lines" to a bedtime,
if thought, and worked through -- could be worthy;
a somewhat unclear nucleus of, what cold be, a good construct,
if thought -- pondered, dremth into -- and worked toward a
full conclusion --

early April, 2015

Season of Thought

To be awake, to know the hour,
to have an awareness of self, of one's own person –
brings, then, a lovely season of thought, almost
to rival the passing of nature's seasons –
passing, quietly and graceful, Chrysanthemums smiling
beneath farewelling, sprightly Crepe Myrtle, scattered florets.
And in the magic of this energy, fleshly being in leftover
summer's tint of gold, the self, aware of
time and seasonal blossoms – the hour bears a full sense of immediacy,
•how not to keep from our hour of ease that in these
selves we express the realities which, bound together,
give complete to our being, our very existence.
To be alone is a curse and yet a respite, to impoverish
and replenish, but always to lead to a sensitivity
to all in conscious perception – or may be – that not conscious.
Being, then, is more blessed than converse, for in it,
yet, with the curse, becomes the impetus to act,
to feel, to embrace sentiment which, somewhere, in its repertoire,
finds hope.

Elizabeth
in deepest night
October 8, 2014

"As Good"

Easy comes, the way of the moment --
all colorings, soundings -- movements --
full reality becomes, is -- of the awareness we
suddenly and reluctantly, if with
satisfaction, follow the waking into, almost as if now
metamorphosed into a planned, if small eternity -- one
which somehow rests in expected place, as if following preludes,
propers, charms -- and halos lighted, with descriptive directives
to become officer to spontaneous responses, having
always been in vintage royalty, of highborn lineage, ever,
and with septres and crowns beside.
-- very being, and in its full recognition, is, if quickly passing,
eventually classic hedonia, the pleasure
giving impetus to movement, together with competition,
birthing critical observation, and, often, unwise conclusion --
bold, we become, in trysts with these small
recognitions -- even yet, to find ourselves
upon the wall, tenuously, in suggestion of the
egg's fall.

The matter of insight and knowing is a coin (it coming of reason)
of rare complexion, lighted and shadowed by its
companion self, sentiment;
these, comprised the universal stage, underscoring
one of the early twentieth century, Russian author's
conclusions: no matter the tense of awareness -- then, now, ever --
man, because of his infrequent exchanges with the commodity of
awareness -- fares poorly more often than could be wished:
we are not as good as we know how to be
("The Father" A. Chekhov).

Those variables which contribute to the "good aware" need be
acceptance when recognized (out whatever fashion), loved
and utilized in daily portions. Then -- if we can
not always be "as good as we know how to
be" -- perhaps the mark might be
to make effort, to approach "as good as we know...."

Elizabeth
-- just at midnight, Good Friday of another Holy Week, passed --
a beautiful day of gratitude and praise
April 3-4, 2015
-- Richard's seventy-second birthday --

Death's Circle
(a round of gold)

Perhaps, somehow, in an apparition's fashion --
yet in guises of every day,
some, especially fated,
will become more in death than in life,
prescribed, or -- with a courtesy of rarravaris carat,
favored an even harvest, extraordinaire.
There is no superlative to the majestic salutation
to life -- gods and goddesses hold well
such true -- not a Sodom, one, commands, for
every quality and carrier, and not yet, one,
with Excaliber's strength, before his
quickly dimming, has to wield the septre that could bear the weight
of all (Everyman).
Death is like a golden band which houses all of the wealth its
circumference allows, in its coming: the realities, the dreams,
the moment, itself, of being -- the ever-spoken fable,
the hard recordings, and the sighs that hold the
moments of tender sentiment which are --
understandably -- unfortunately, without, in
description.
A halo will extend, a shadow constrict; the glint of the
piercing sun, startling, open; but the band, still has all that
the verb "to be" can whisper or sigh --
or weep into still -- within its span.
And only in death, these other, all, reductionists, can
only -- "it" -- in all bright and softness -- hold
complete, the present in one moment of loss.

When youth has lived, flown its jubilant sky paths,
there flies, then, beside, a spirit, a loss, like
a great, feathered bird whose raven has
given over to silver,
the lovely weight-bearing all to the below, but all will,
in this once, be glorious,
more, in the review.

As Cleopatra's phrase of Antony's horse sang
beauty of its weight to bear --
metaphorically --
singular, cognitive awareness, the less that fits inside
the circle's glow: full-mooned.

Elizabeth
July 30, 2015, eleven o'clock pm

-- the above prose verse was
prompted by re-reading some of lines marked of Faulkner's work --
beautiful, harsh, true to the mark of the grand
paradox we all are,
and unhappily affords players of ourselves, until --
someone offers, in the light of gifted reason,
someone -- who sees our particular,
own self -- true -- throughout the entire
cosmos -- as we strew, and fetch,
wander, yet, our own, our very own, steps.

I feel my loneliness recently, more than my dependency --
overly much, and I can only reach, to hold nothing,
nothing --

Elizabeth Afterthought

Medicinal Choice

Spring is in, and the hours are nearing
Maundy Thursday;
and yet, in my small cosem, my humble fiefdom,
there is no accounting of hours.
The clever pirate, time, unending, but
always closing – my hours, my individual
parcels of time – have abruptly, though in adroit,
insidiously unhurried steps, closed,
not of my will, but surely of circumstance.
Memory, out the halls of yesterday, offers sentiment,
and nourishment, but, by their very acquiescing to
the pirate, can propose no tomorrows,
only empty dreams – a long road of
shadow, clouds, mists, and an apparition, perhaps.
The feast cannot be accessed, if yet, the journey
not concluded;
without voice or touch, or exchanges which continue the processing,
the face of God, the grande Natural, with the great,
cathedraled hall of the past – these compose my only
garden in which to see life:
blossoms which call forth smiles into tears,
wounding within fragrance, unapproachable hues
alongside brightness, rainbowed;
I hold the life I can have, it a peaceful psalm
at every eventide, my companion, my guest –
beautiful solitude – if janused – ushered in by
circumstance occasioned by the
medicinal ingredient of choice.

Elizabeth
at twilight
April 16, 2014
thoughts, evaluating the realities I perceive –

Cameo Moment

In a cameo moment, under the stylus of night's
darkened quiet and still –
and added to, perhaps, the space between
the length of one and another heartbeat, only just a petal
softness, but enough, so that all intuit – somehow – suppose, to
survive – further, that beauty, its
integrity, its honor and constancy, its eternis of,
in some fashion, fragmentation but empowerment with
warmth and care – this celestial phenomenon
embraces all, to aesthetically charm and please, to
suggest, yet, further wisdom, to salute, to commemorate, the
blessedness of all things.
If such adventure in thought be gifted us, we forget our
murmurings, and cleave to our own, now, portion
of salvation: we stand "lesser gods," without abashment,
into full fraternity.

The violin string, taunt to touch; the distance of
stars, speaking with their light variations;
the turn of the calendar, and an immediate ambiance of a
new season – of gold and cool, of life and
death – into new life –
ah, the boon of immortal constancy, yet that of the
combination of the delay and the petal's
caesura – the impetus toward the
absolute glory of the reigning heartbeat;
beast, beast that I am, and my heart, my
heart, that I love; bitter, bitter

that you give, but mine, love of that I hold –
for thou art alone, mine, and
in thee, we represent life. Blessed is the
igniting of my worthy knowing, it to
flower, into the larger truth, the magnanimous
gift of grace.

Elizabeth
in deepest night
August 3-4, 2014

the "beast" analogy can be referenced to one of Stephen Crane's short
verses, it, of a small collection, powerfully
written, in his short, tubercular
life – with other notable works – salute!

– written while passing over into sleep –

Untruthful Regret

My heart bears the pain of emptiness,
but as if it will burst with tears falling long, and long, and long.
My hands hold no warmth, none to lay touch,
still, long, and long, and long.
The wretchedness of my full shell is transparent,
for no filling rests there.
All of my loves have gone away – in defense,
or by being pushed apart – but more, and alone,
fullest still – forgotten.
Cana's elegantly beautiful pomegranate, in its blush of rose
and fuchsia, a touch of rouge and quieted gold – it
has no truth of its coming sunken cheeks
and lacking of former, pleasing hues –
yet, berries of springtime, hanging, dew-laden, to
become motionless, umbered brown foundlings,
now lifeless – once sweet purple with violet smiles of light.
these – my companions in the glory of late
summer, yet more, the full of coming winter.

"the way of all flesh..."
S. Maugham

True courage lies in remembering without regret.

Elizabeth
thoughts of a pensive "lesser" god –
December, second week, 2014

Confused Sentiments

The progress of days is most the lifting about
of our "importances;"
some gather as those lovely, verses and
touch, steps of resolve and faith;
hands that yield roads, cradles, yet a
formidable cathedral.
Others bide the dark of unspoken thought,
and sentiment, out glimpses with movement
toward and away – while some press in, truly, directions
unknown to even he who pushes forth,
the press in, often, quite different direction from
the obviously required.
Still, as creatures of being – isness – spirit and flesh,
we strive for constancy, and if not,
reconciliation into a compatible arrangement.
Together is born a sweetness and a sadness,
our efforts with our importances, our skill
at compatibility inferior to that of dissonance.
Oh day, give all of thy properties of
good to us, the seekers of good, if holding,
at times, dark centers;
allow us to laugh into the sunlight, to venture
toward an ultimate peace; to mediate
our circumstance into plowshares,
and to stand and reflect, bowing in gratitude.

Elizabeth
in late night, bittersweet sentiments too confused to label
September 7, 2014

Thoughts at Twilight

In truth, the full glory in any prize we clasp, into
holding, we have brought, most, ourselves.

– on discipline, perseverance, fulfillment – significance –

– Since all is a very flow, pressed forward by
circumstance, with perception, alongside the factor of
individual relativity – including will – these significant
properties of living play hard roles in our
thought formulation of a weltanschauung – within, and some
because of, the "mind mass:" how other can
we reason of "things" –

And awareness plays out its particulars, of flowers and a garden gate,
or the subway and hanging, stale air. We, then, the "I," the "me"
of the awareness think that we see patterns, coincidences,
anniversaries – something more, something of us – but the reality,
and it only a moment to most of us, was the unfolding of will
and circumstance, time the great equalizer, fitting "all" into
a grande histoire.
Even then, still, if the history is not spoken or read, it will perish
with the dew fall, the twilight, the collection which we
were; if the record of selected particulars is kept, and
somehow made known, we will live another moment, but only a
moment, more, to finally perish anew, for the wait of
another who may add, or take away, he, too, to perish
into the wait.
The sum, of "it all," is that the cognizance we
hold, in a moment – is our being –
to make more, with record or no – becomes surmise.

As much as forethought, responsible insuring, projection out studies of
standing realities – the moment is, in reason
and sentiment, paramount
in the "business" of living; and it passes, changes, inviting
"adjustment," metamorphosing, the moment's death within its
own life. We do well to cultivate memory for ourselves, and for
a short time, others, that our "glory" live and increase, if only
within a comprehensible period. Ought else is acceptance, with the
forward appendage of thought – hope.

Myth, fable and such help, but we fetter their
usefulness in pushing, pressing
their similarities to ourselves, therefore lessening the true power they
could wield. Perhaps it is in each consciousness that there lies the
explanation we all seek – only to be realized,
however undocumented,
at the time of most necessity.

The flight of birds, the constancy of the seasons, the realities
of memory and forgetfulness – these are concrete entities,
and substantiate the myth of our being. It is the echo, the
cognitive halos that dress our days, which add the poignancy
of what we concept as life. The poignancy is sweet, and it is
sad, and perhaps we can attribute much of the
disorganization, the fragmenting of our era to
advanced technology, it yielding "creature comforts"
and "big" information – so that time has

been found for the pressing of present, unfortunate
issues – the pastoral antidote is
distant, and undervalued in its innocence and simplicity –
finds then, dismantled, our societal structure, once,
more in place for very real needs. It may be
that the great irony of our dilemma is the sacrificing
of all freedom so that we may have
some, and the, always again, more.

Elizabeth
thoughts at twilight
April 4, 2014
Richard's seventy-first birthday

The Dream of Lost Victory

Waking a second time, and sleep heavy of dreams,
sweet, of deepest pain --
passion, spent, glory lost, wisdom taunting --
ah, master of words -- "... et je pleure."
Lifting out the distant nocturnal land, then lovely
gardens and left images, burked by progress
of the processing day, the window to feasts, those
of yesterday --
full, sumptuously filled of joy - lost to must be to the
window of today -- these first comfort, and wound,
unmercifully, for they can, but only more,
repeat the law of those in whose station we may
not remain -- but we, now, are -- cognizant of loss, to stay or
depart -- we "lesser gods."
And yet, when the spider's lace, beside the mists of quieting,
kept thought retires to the dark of truest knowing,
We embrace the visiting of life, each full into the
open window out which one dreams of then,
but, most, of now, below in early grasses, and the beauty of lands
of grails, to which we travel while light allows; still, the new feast
arranges, calling with invitations and status
appointed -- and we must stay as long as we may, but the
circles, whatever their origins or kind, come over and
again into themselves --
ever, always, now into all time -- by the road, the path
of many -- ever victorious, but lost.

Elizabeth
-- written during the months of my most recent illness -- pain, heavy
medication, often rousing for moments in the night to
write; some of the transcription may be unclear--
transcribed tonight, May 3, 2015
near nine o'clock pm

Uncertain Lines

In pleasant review, how glorious,
within every forgetfulness of
the feast of day –
yet, further, the contented self, these, all, being embraced by the
grace of night.
Reason and spirit come together in a
closeness and permitted distance;
"together" connotes "getting to," and with
the casual expression, it rings
courtesies and warmth, and whispers – and
in each of us, brings a presence.
In fullest paths, with blessed steps, I, yet, am so,
and feel we are each not a scholar,
but know of wonder, enhanced.
Oh glory, beauty in splendor –
the warmth, the vibrant Rose, the patient Sunflower,
with brilliantly scarlet Geranium, alongside –
to close in acquiescence is but the sleep of gods,
that of alternate gold, and
beside earthly coinage, having
no parameters.

Sunrise into moon glow;
innocence into knowing:
all as one –

Elizabeth
in deepest night
July 16-17, 2014

– my pen arriving to lines of which I an not certain,
other than the joy in being given life –

– read these lines as they take on feeling, and
punctuation will arrange –

Dark Flowers

Dark flowers, those which come into
their full, complete selves when there is
no light,
perhaps most appropriately at the midnight
hour, and, most appropriately, they to become dark Roses –
these lovely creatures do not must to
carry evil as a property, either in being,
or intention, in hue or fragrance.
Howso, then, is this construct assessed –
by empirical evidence in early morning's light –
these Roses lie lifeless – beautiful in manner indescribable,
with fragrance as chaste as the jeweled belt, yet, fastened –
and, in form and hue, incomparable to
any showing in the sun's smile.
A self cannot be the object of comparison or
judgment, and must hold her most true
being within, until it is truly free:
to herself, only, is she the object of evaluation, for
others, merely a glimpse, and a surmise;
the world's poverty of the dark Rose, in days of one
sun, or that of an eon's – will provide for the riddle –
and if no one learns of the answer, the dark
Rose lies, moves, – was, is – in some manner –
content.

Elizabeth
August 10, 2014

Every self (heart), lighted or dark, within the
scope of its awareness, is its own person,
and knows, at some level, its place in the finding of the balance.
That spoken of here is *ultimate, final judgment,* a concept which is
truly inconceivable to man – the full circle
would need be seen and understood;
We do, then, the best that we can, and try to
live, well, together, failing as often
as we succeed. This verse is only a "pointer" in individual
relationships – from our perspective – Divine
Providence, whatever Its Nature,
will, of course, lead, and ultimately see
that "all is well" with each soul.

Balance Concluded

I will carry, always, the weight
of my loss,
but my hurt, not anymore, heavy, it having died
in the conscious forgetting to remember.
The death -- slowly, slowly,
having perished in the emptiness of
remembrance, permitted the sentence of Sarto's truth to emptiness --
the death -- insidiously creeping, successfully,
accomplished within the
completeness of time, it, in busy unawareness,
and being uncultivated -- allowed
the arrival of time without --
unable to add, or to forgive --
withered, with no moist -- into the away:
the balance, in full departure.

Elizabeth
in deepest night, an appropriate hour for
just such awarenesses --
March 7, 2015

"Perhaps there strikes a balance."

The reference to "Sarto." is from a character
often drawn into my pieces;
Robert Browning, the one of two major British poets of the
Victorian Period draws Sarto as one of his major characters in the
verse "Andrea del Sarto," a painter whose beautiful, unfaithful wife
always comes back to him -- his caring wish
giving purpose to his continuing --
a scenario we all face at times --

The "riddle." oftentimes, with appropriate space and thought,
turns back on itself -- in the clarity of full
observation, appraisal, into conclusion.

-- an "Elizabeth hypothetical"
afterthought -
gone with the wind,

Elizabeth

in deepest night, the appropriate hour for
just such coming awarenesses --
March 6, 2015

Fabled True

Wheels are in the far distance in these hours,
and in my rooms, quiet halos
the bloom of lamps;
the key has stood lieutenant to the mammoth
wood, protecting the honored of
its keep;
winds, though frigid, as evidenced by walking
past undraped glass,
serve to increase the warmth of thought in my
familiar, if metamorphosed, hearth.
Ah, how sweet these moments of giving awareness,
as distant from unfortunate angst
as consequences to first lovers.
When these such moments visit our thoughtful whole,
the past becomes an enamored quest,
tomorrow, a beautiful unknowing -- and this moment --
in gracious sentiment, as murmurings of
the heart of the fatther, embracing his lost son --
their wealthy lineage, together, in a moment
allowing the joy of all awareness, when that
which was adverse, without, now blessed by a
golden cord of memory, within: from fatigue of indulgence, to
love, once, and more, giving courage to come,
to bow and to be loved:
the grail we all wish to hold, still, to
bless and honor, redemptive love and extended
peace.

Elizabeth
-- a moment of contentment, if in fantasy;
good fatigue, cognizant of multiples of good, blessing my
coming sleep --

January 16, 2015

Call With Thy Voice

Sleep with me a good sleep,
and gather my lamentations into a
wineskin of many, thoughtful flavors,
A very fold under Thy staff;
dream to me of the beautiful, of the
embroidery of my days:
the blue of sky,
the green earth,
and rose Rose, the color my mother
gave to me.
And when I am refreshed, call as with Thy
very voice to Samuel,
to rise, and with purposed steps, enter into
the promising invitation
of new, waiting day.

Elizabeth
just before sleep
September 4, 2014

Worded Absolution

The day's fullness was passed, and in its new emptiness, the
solitude of its hours joined those of its completion.
I looked, and felt, I listened and I found all of
nothing, my heart in deep longing for dialogue, for observing,
expressing and receiving.
But found only was the constancy of silence of listening
hearts which could not, somehow, close the arc.
I, in fullest, frenetic motion, must to move, be, in some fashion,
to break the dark glass that encompassed my soul.
I forgave my reason, and fell to my senses, finding after
fullest images and feeling, a sense of warmth, and the color of
live flame, passions of all varieties.
In heaviness of breath, I felt a rock, hard, mis-
shapened, but in my fire, becoming
intractable, in lovely contours.
Enough, -- no-- yet more, for I, in
nourishment was yet clean of filling.
-- looking, listening, I still heard no more; still and still
I listened, and thought a sigh, or more a tear, flowing, like
dark, comforting waters.
And with all of the strength of Samson, my hair flowing
out of captivity, I listened with my most inner, my most impotent
ear -- and I heard words.
I was granted, then, within absolute grace,
worded absolution.

When my moods are down, and I must to break the stay, I do not know where the impetus to do so arises -- but it does, to be repeated over and over again. The pain is always newly intense, and all that I can know is that prayers of my own, and those who have, and do, love me ignite the fire, bring forth the shoot, bringing back the glory into glory; most, I think I know it is the consideration of grace, a benevolence I do not fully understand.

Sentiment/reason executing, together, are a kind of Penelope/Dido arrangement. Cool, and gentle thought, in true care against impulsive, if beautifully passionate sensibilities, but indolent composing of a necessary conclusion draw a very divergent image. We need both varieties of reason and sentiment, but neither, alone. Semantics, with limitations, agreed, offer to help us as gregarious animals. We must have our solitude, to learn what it does not "say." -- some more than others -- less the animal -- And all beauty and sentiment cannot be expressed verbally, but only felt in the/between the hearts -- or in some other symbolical fashion: we "lesser gods" do, without speculation -- of any mode -- require dialogue, that mortal, and immortal.

Elizabeth
September 20, 2015
long day, down --

Small Meditations, Near Sleep

Most Holy God, Thou whose turns extend
toward
thy benefaction,
I pray Thy indulgence for brightest
care, over my surest drape,
as I wait Holy Presence, leaving a larger,
and more balancing of, being.

– smoke from falling, gray pearls, onto
a waiting breast –
And I am in the smoke, and wish to
lie upon Thy breast, knowing
the security of many, accepting
souls.

– within the climbing Moonflower, it expressing
the soft, summer's moonface – moonface
kiss my needing,
a waiting, vessel, without – all,
of The Master's fashioning.

And kindly Shadow, spread Thy
lighted darkness over me,
that the dancing of measured reason
cast about, a peace.

Elizabeth
late evening-early morning, December 5-6, 2013

These small prayers were partially written near coming, heavy sleep;
the script is difficult to understand, and I have improvised,
somewhat –

refashioned and scripted, early 2014

Two Images

My thought bears the weight
of the disc,
collecting all of its being,
just before lifting to
freedom.
And in the fellowship of thought,
comes, now, the image
of early morning –
the heavy lifting, slowly, slowly,
of the moon, full, fair, of the noblesse, through
a giving window,
but with practiced certainty, into its down.
"The moon is down," and
thought wings, the lark in its
efitely being, self – how else to find new day, but so given into the
presence of self, out heaviness and prescribed
law – into the beauty of openness,
movement – joyful being.

Elizabeth
March 25, 2014
– near eight-fifteen, resting from chores –
Spring and Easter are already ours.

– recalling two images in these breakfast hours, as the sun spreads its
glory into the all of day: the disc near midnight, when effort at
sleep was great, and later, several hours, at glancing
out, to see the lifting of the moon into the away –
The world of the Natural sings always to me, my constant keeper
of beauty, and truth – not at all judgmental, but as much
so, real.

To Sing Again

The frightened, fragile, and-- inside its world –
the very small bird has visited again –
as if no refuge were ever in place before,
and storms quieted about it in its flight.
Refuge is again in place, and the storms quieted, and thee, thee
litte bird is found neglectful of the certainty
of the promise given the sparrow.
Can the heart of all that lives know love enough,
divine or mortal, not to be fearful –
trees, dwellings, health and fortune remain
through days and seasons, through thought unclear and
confused – to become a happy sameness,
the familiar we love.
Andso – where flies our constancy, and firm stance, our staid
resolve: the rose is compatible with its thorn, the
day into night, the leaf with gold on one
side, only.
Our lives must plead the self to seek its refuge at the
center, to stay the distance by observing,
offering prayers; by recounting historical events –
by remembering the curve of our mother's arm.
To fear is to die a small death, over again, but to be
thoughtful in our awareness, dependent, in our faith –
to hope in our strength – surely the frightened little
bird will sing again, in whatever climes or the
circumstance of its being.

Elizabeth
in deepest night
September 11, 2014

Toward Eternal Climes

-- the day, the day -- now in its dark side,
its mysterious -- its apparitions and visions of truth --
but in its bright, its continuous issue of the voice
of life, truth was clearer, nearer, more beautiful and less
ambiguous -- if more untrue, and more a crude
raw -- as dead flesh in its first moments
without breath, if poignantly beautiful to its receiving.
How do we decipher the most true of the verities we perceive;
perhaps through looking -- looking past
foreboding -- denial, or with what death we
can, looking into its eyes to find
the drape pulled aside.
The journey into a day, from rising to lying
down, is a generous enigma
whose wisdom does not present, perhaps, until darkness
covers particulars that distract, distort, tease and offer
the obtuse in the face of reason -- when their personae of
assistance (clarity, insight) drift into the nothingness
of "Well, whatever."
Truth is the difficult given, and of life it is the pondering hurt
reviewing the beauty with the beast; the answer allows
the peace of sleep, the opportunity to free levels of, then,
conscious thought through which Divine insight
permits -- all the more -- presses, to ponder,
to, further, in seeking anguish
find ultimate understanding that will,
without fear, in the final turn, (no arms or legs crossed, prostrate
on the receiving earth, inside cries of mercy), let steps process through
to eternal climes.

Elizabeth
the first days of September
in deepest night, when my pen pulls forth
my voice of deepest, inner thought
2015
The example of the fallen warrior, begging
mercy is familiar to Medieval students of
literature; -- if the fallen's arms and legs were crossed, lying
prostrate on the soil, and begging for mercy -- if this such
occasion occurred, the horsed (the victor) warrior was bound
to allow the fallen to live; in the story of Turnus, the fallen was
not spared, but brutally "run through." -- *The Aeneid* --

Of Certainty and Finality

The day is quickly, now, giving up its light,
and shadowings, in their graciously gentle press,
assure the close presence of night.
As is with love and friendship, the ebbing and tiding
of days always arrives, again, to
a beginning.
There is a comfort in certainty, yet a disturbing
finality – if wanted or no –
and we poor, creatures of the moment,
employ whatever is at hand to disguise this holding construct:
a deferring amazement at blossoms out of season,
the Southern pear in autumn's bloom; elders
who insist their youth – but more likely, we find thinking in
patterns which celebrate the wishes we
hold, with denying and extending – these suggest instruments helping
secure our various angst – as with music, color, and fragrance:
the lengthy scroll of history and literature, and the wealth of kin
and friend – all very prayers within our hearts
for relief of that we cannot suffer to ultimately be.
The provision of yesterday, and the fanciful
we draw into our tomorrows,
are truly shields to the strength of present realities since our hearts
desire to be in the moment's pleasure, alone; the roll call
of strategies is legion: pleasantries, which fulfill our plethora of needs,
the escaping of fearful circumstances – each serves as the lighted
candle in a darkened room, engendering our most helpful
sentiment – hope – as it is in place beside faith, that far
beyond doctrine or writ.

Perhaps, then, the beauty of the evening star, the duet of responsibility
and accomplishment, provided by the day's gold – these might
tender our sentiments regarding that which
cannot be altered. Added to, can be
the appointment of rouge to summer's
Rose; the catch of our breath in
winter's chill; the bravely kind eulogy; the unwilling "must"
glance to a gift of one no longer present –
these could become worthy exchanges for
the certainties, and finalities
we will, with the existential of tense, know.
 – *the pattern in an old world rug,*
 the ocean resting in its tranquil blue;
 brilliant hickory gold in Southern autumns,
 a familiar smile of recognition on reaching harbor –
 our lives fill, over, and over, again
 with beauty, truth and fraternity –
 ought else but to peacefully
 give over the day –
 Elizabeth, at twilight, June 1, 2014
 -- in answer to, once, Dr. Norton's retort --

Rumi's Tribute

Oh ancient, Eastern singer,
wordsmith of true passion:
my unmeasured gratitude for your
voicing the ability of the All Good --
in circled, complete,
of purist, weighted gold --

to give the greatest more, to enlarge possible
goodness in all, bringing
oneness of mortal creation --
there becoming,

oneness,
into togetherness,
within the shadow of Thy step,

the absolute grace of *transcendence*.

Elizabeth
December 13, 2015
at dew fall

a response to reading the love poems of Rumi,
three sittings, begun, December 12, 2015
Christmastime

Peace

Peace

Eulogy

from the death of St John the Hut Dweller

"He has simply pitched his tent in another direction."

a partial line from one of Elizabeth's verses, "At Times,":

...the drape of
...the past is slipping into a well-earned content,
if one without and with; going home is reaching the
comfortable forward --

an eternis conclusive

OTHER WORKS BY
ELIZABETH CLAYTON:

I, Elizabeth
2007

Songs from the Eleventh Month
2008

A Thousand White Gardenias
2009

Unto Relationship
2009

Musings
2009

La libelule
2010

Chanson de Harold
2011

Shenandoah Songs
2012

The Sun and Geranium Poems
2012

Scarlet Flow
2012

The Myth of Being
2015

The Quiet Sheba trilogy
2015-2016

Printed in the United States
By Bookmasters